We Had A Job To Do

WE HAD A
JOB TO DO

A BASIC HISTORY OF WORLD WAR II
THROUGH THE EYES OF THOSE WHO SERVED

THERESA ANZALDUA

Interior design by Caitlin Bechtel
Cover design by Kristin Bryant

Printed by Harvard Book Store
1256 Massachusetts Ave.
Cambridge, Massachusetts 02138

Table of Contents

Preface

Hundreds of thousands of people experienced, reported upon and have studied World War II, and there are many interpretations of and disagreements over the war's events. The information in this book is based on official U.S. government documents and interviews with veterans conducted by the author. Gabriel Reid Crumpler, a life-long student of World War II, provided the fact check for this book. He encourages readers to look into some of the countless books and websites that delve into and analyze the many controversies and debates about nearly every aspect of the war.

This photograph of a migrant worker named Florence Owens Thompson is a part of Photographer Dorothea Lange's work documenting the Great Depression for the U.S. Farm Security Administration. The iconic photo, taken in February of 1936, is known as "Migrant Mother" and as "Destitute Pea-Picking Family in Depression."
Photo courtesy of the Franklin D. Roosevelt Library Public Domain Photographs.

The Great Depression, Prelude to War and the Service of Private First Class Salvatore Santoro, U.S. Army

At age one hundred, Salvatore Santoro sits at his kitchen table, runs his hands through his thick head of hair and takes a phone call from his stockbroker concerning a recent stock purchase he has made. Hanging up the phone, he explains his investment in the East Boston Savings Bank and then describes how he decided to serve in World War II because of the Great Depression. The era, he says, shaped his life in many ways. Born in 1914 in Boston's North End, Santoro was fifteen years old on October 29, 1929, a day known as "Black Tuesday," when the U.S. stock market crashed. With the crash, the house-of-cards economy of the 1920's -- the "Roaring Twenties" -- toppled, and the U.S. went into economic free fall.

Santoro will never forget the Great Depression. "There were no jobs," he says, sadly, "I lost ten years of my life." When stock prices plummeted on Black Tuesday, a downward spiral began. Banks failed when bad loans they had made to stock speculators went unpaid. When the failed banks closed their doors, bank deposits – which in that era were still uninsured – disappeared, and millions of hardworking people lost all their savings. As Americans lost their money and their spending slowed, businesses cut back production and laid off workers.

America's farm families – then nearly one-third of the U.S. population – had expanded their operations during World War I and as a result were producing surplus crops, causing prices to plummet, and they were carrying too much debt. With a massive drought and the Dust Bowl storms thrown into the mix, farms failed in droves, as did the banks whose loans they could not re-pay.

During the Depression, Santoro served for three years in the National Guard, attended college to study finance and did find work here and there, but nothing that took advantage of his skills or that he could build a life around. At the beginning of 1929, before the crash, 1.5 million heads of households, mainly men, were unemployed. By 1932, 12 million workers were out of jobs. "It was very, very bad. There were soup kitchens, and nobody was working. I couldn't even buy a cup of coffee and a donut because that was ten cents. I just hung around. I'll never forget it. It was horrible," Santoro remembers.

Many people were ashamed about being poor and out of work during the Depression, and many committed suicide. The suicide rate tripled between 1929 and 1933. Santoro was able to keep his spirits up. "I hung on, hung on, hung on," he explains. He eventually found a job in horticulture, through a government program, and put himself through college. In early 1940, after war had broken out overseas, President Franklin Delano Roosevelt called upon U.S. manufacturers to start building airplanes and other war supplies. In a radio address to the American people – a "fireside chat" – on May 26, 1940, Roosevelt spoke sadly about the war in Europe and encouraged citizens and businesses to support America's national defense effort. He told businesses that the government "stands ready to advance the necessary money to help provide for the enlargement of factories, the establishment of new plants, the employment of thousands of necessary workers…." Like so many people who had suffered through the Depression, Santoro finally was able to find decent work in the national defense effort.

Santoro made it through the Depression and later, after the U.S. entered the war, he operated a lathe at the Watertown Arsenal, an important Army munitions factory outside of Boston. He hated every minute of his job. Santoro has a mind for business and didn't like to work with his hands. He wanted to help in the war effort, but he needed a good job and training upon which to base a career. When his boss put him on the midnight shift, he just had to quit. The U.S. Army Major who ran the factory tried to talk him out of it, but Santoro told him there was no way he was going to work midnights as a lathe operator. Santoro decided that his best route to a good job was to join the military.

An Executive Order had ended voluntary enlistment in December of 1942, so getting drafted was the only way to get inducted into the military. Santoro had not been drafted, but he wasn't going to let that stand in his way. In June of 1944, Santoro went to the local draft board and told a woman who worked there that he had quit his job and had a wife and two daughters. "You've got to put me on the list to be drafted," he demanded. She told Santoro absolutely not, that she was not permitted to do such a thing. Santoro was determined, however. All that summer he stopped by the local draft board, and eventually he got his way. In October, with the fellows at the draft board telling him that he "must be some kind of a nut," they agreed to take someone else's name off the draft list – someone who probably never knew how lucky he was – and drafted Santoro instead. Suffering through all the years of the Great Depression had left Santoro determined to get himself established financially and support his family to the best of his abilities. He had succeeded in getting himself drafted and was sent to serve in Europe as the war was winding down and so did not run much risk of becoming a casualty in war, but he did have a couple of close calls surviving the dangerous aftermath of war-torn Europe.

Private First Class Santoro's story continues in Chapter 20.

Children sitting outside of what was their home in London, England, in September of 1940, after a German bomb attack in the Battle of Britain. Photo courtesy of the U.S. National Archives, number 306-NT-3163V.

The World Goes to War
The Service of Sergeant Clayton ("Bill") Cooke, U.S. Army

The Great Depression started to wind down as the U.S. began building war supplies for its longtime friend and ally, England. England and France had declared war on Germany in late 1939 after Germany invaded Poland, marking the start of World War II in Europe. World War II in the Pacific had started two years earlier, in 1937, when Japan invaded another friend of the United States – China.

By late 1940, with the U.S. manufacturing war equipment for England and for the U.S. national defense, the economy was on the rise. Jesse Jones, the U.S. Secretary of Commerce, announced that factory payrolls were the highest since 1929. Americans had money to spend, and they enjoyed themselves. Most Americans went to the movies fairly regularly, and there they could see video footage of the wars being fought in Europe, Asia and Africa. The ships, planes, and bombed-out cities shown in the newsreels were terribly sad to see – and thankfully very far away.

England faced a huge threat from Germany, and Americans were happy to help supply England with equipment, but not with troops. Many Americans felt strongly isolationist and were determined to stay out of war. American troops were drafted and trained to protect the U.S. homeland, as a part of the national defense program. At home, people read about the massive amounts of war supplies the U.S. was producing under the program and gazed in awe at magazine photographs of magnificent military equipment -- rows of shining airplane propellers, lines of gleaming airplanes. The size and sheer numbers of the munitions in the photos were dazzling – children cut out the photos and collected them. People were proud of the technology under production in the U.S., particularly after having just lived through the gloomy years of the Great Depression.

As Thanksgiving of 1941 approached, factories that normally made consumer goods were being retooled and were manufacturing military equipment. The weight of the Depression was lifting more and more. At around this time some Americans began to notice press reports of increased Japanese military activity in the Pacific Ocean, but most folks, if they noticed, dismissed Japan as a small country capable of little more than manufacturing cheap, tin toys, knock-offs of superior, American-made goods.

The Thanksgiving edition of *The Saturday Evening Post*, one of the country's most popular magazines, appeared on newsstands across America on November 22. The cover photo, by Richard Miller, featured a little girl peeking up from her hands folded in prayer, eyeing the roasted turkey on the Thanksgiving table while her family says grace. Americans were thankful.

Several days after Thanksgiving, on Sunday, December 7, 1941, people were enjoying the beginning of the holiday season. Retailers considered Thanksgiving to be the official beginning of the Christmas shopping season, and chambers of commerce across the country had towns and cities decorated for Christmas. The U.S. was a largely Christian country, and most Americans observed Sundays as a Sabbath day of rest and quiet relaxation. On December 7, people went to church, enjoyed special Sunday dinners with their families and went on "Sunday drives" in enormous cars. Friends chipped in for gas that cost about twelve cents a gallon. In New York City, people shopped, went to the movies and strolled by the Christmas decorations. The New York Giants played the Brooklyn Dodgers in a football game at the New York Polo Grounds.

A three-hour drive away from New York, Clayton ("Bill") Cooke was enjoying a typical, December Sunday at home in West Hartford, Connecticut. He, his two brothers, and their father were reading the big Sunday edition of the newspaper. A section of comics or "funny papers," which kids and adults enjoyed, could be found in the middle of the paper. "Flash Gordon," "Blondie," and "Barney Google and Snuffy Smith" were popular. The Cookes were gathered around their radio, a beautiful piece of furniture, listening to programs as they read. Radio provided all kinds of information and entertainment – dramas, comedies, news, sports, weather and music.

Suddenly, at 2:30 p.m. Eastern Standard Time, the major radio networks across the country interrupted regular programming for a special news bulletin. Japan had attacked the U.S. Naval base at Pearl Harbor, in the U.S. territory of Hawaii. Bill Cooke, the eldest of the three brothers, was lying on the floor in the living room, listening to the radio and reading the funny papers. He couldn't believe his ears. The attack had begun more than an hour earlier and was still in progress as the announcement was made. The Japanese were bombing Americans.

Word spread across the country. Some people burst into tears when they heard the news. The attack surely meant that America would go to war. Countless people uttered the words, "Our lives will never be the same." The West Coast of the U.S. was ordered to black out all light that evening, so people there spent the day covering their windows. People at movies, shops and football games sought the safety of home.

All across the country, stunned and saddened Americans sat by their radios with their families and friends and listened as details of the ongoing attack unfolded. More than three thousand Americans stationed at the U.S. base at Pearl Harbor were killed or wounded. The U.S. Pacific fleet was crippled. Cooke didn't know where Pearl Harbor was, and his father told him to look it up in the family's atlas. Many Americans looked up Pearl Harbor that day, in their atlas or their family encyclopedia, because most of them had never heard of it. Cooke was astonished by the radio reports of the losses the U.S. endured. He soon found out that most of the U.S. Navy's fleet was at Pearl Harbor. The U.S. government, struggling with Japan diplomatically and having noticed Japan's increasing military build-up in the Pacific, had stationed most of the U.S. Naval fleet at Pearl Harbor as a show of strength.

Never in a million years did Cooke think that he would end up fighting in the Pacific, but he did. Cooke was seventeen years old and like many other boys in the U.S. he was about to become a soldier, fight in a war, and grow up fast.

The day after Pearl Harbor, President Roosevelt announced in an address to Congress that December 7, 1941, would be "a date which will live in infamy," and the U.S. formally declared war against Japan. Three days later, Germany and Italy, which, had allied with Japan as the Axis Powers, declared war on the United States. The U.S. was now fully embroiled in World War II, leading the Allied Powers with Great Britain and, nominally, Soviet Russia.

When Bill Cooke's father told him to look up Pearl Harbor in the family atlas, he knew his boy would have to go off to war. Cooke's childhood was soon to end, and it had been a good one, even though he had grown up during the Depression. Cooke's father had owned a nightclub out in the country -- a roadhouse -- on Bantam Lake in Morris, Connecticut. When he was a small boy, just as the Roaring 1920's was devolving into the Great Depression, Cooke would help his dad at the Saturday night parties at the roadhouse. The club girls back then were known as "flappers," and Cooke watched them dance with their friends to live jazz music played by musicians and singers who traveled from club to club.

Cooke attended a one-room schoolhouse in Morris, and while his classmates brought lettuce sandwiches for lunch, he had chicken from the roadhouse. People didn't have much money for food during the Depression, so they ate from their gardens. Cooke would trade his chicken sandwiches for the lettuce sandwiches he preferred, and the other children were certainly happy to have something as expensive as chicken for their lunch.

As the Depression deepened during the 1930's and the flamboyant flappers went out of style, Cooke's father gave up the roadhouse and took a job with the Railway Express Agency – the FedEx™ of its day – and moved his family to West Hartford, Connecticut, where Cooke and his brothers attended high school, played sports and listened to the radio.

Soon after Pearl Harbor, Cooke turned eighteen and registered with his local draft board, as required by law. He then waited to see when he would be called up to go to war. He had graduated from Hall High School and was attending Morse Business College when he got his "greeting" from Uncle Sam. Uncle Sam was the stern-looking, grey-bearded man featured in some very popular war campaign posters. A typical poster had Uncle Sam pointing his finger and a caption that read, "Uncle Sam wants you."

Cooke's greeting was the letter he and millions of other young men received from the U.S. government, which began with the word "Greeting," and then stated that their local draft boards had selected them for service and ordered them to report for induction into the military – immediately. A few days after he received his letter, on February 15, 1943, Cooke said goodbye to his family and reported to his draft board. He was sent to Fort Devens in Massachusetts to be processed into the U.S. Army. His civilian clothes were packed up and sent home because he would wear only Army-issued clothes now. He had no idea of what he would be doing in the Army or where he would be sent. He wasn't really frightened to be going off to war – rather, he felt excited to be embarking on an adventure. Fourteen months had passed since he had looked up Pearl Harbor in the atlas.

After Fort Devens, the Army sent Cooke to Fort Bragg, in North Carolina, for basic training and artillery training. The boy from Connecticut was pretty good with his gun, though he had no idea of where he was going to be using it. After completing a couple months of training, Cooke was given his first assignment: to guard German prisoners of war at P.O. Box 1142.

Early in the war, the United States had activated a top-secret intelligence base on part of the grounds of Mount Vernon, the plantation built by George Washington. Located in Virginia, just outside of Washington, D.C., the secret base was known only by its postal abbreviation, P.O. Box 1142, and was demolished when the war ended. P.O. Box 1142 is a fascinating and little-known part of World War II. By the time information about the base became declassified beginning in the 1970's, many of the people who knew of its existence had passed away. Cooke is one of the few people alive who can give a first-hand account of this secret base. The U.S. questioned thousands of important German military officials and scientists at P.O. Box 1142.

During the World War II era, the Germans' scientific and technological prowess was fearsome, particularly in the fields of submarines and rocketry. The intelligence gathered at P.O. Box 1142 was critical to the Allied war effort and even to the Space Race and the Cold War that followed World War II.

After basic and artillery training, Cooke enjoyed traveling to Virginia to the secret base and living on the beautiful grounds of Mount Vernon. One of the few swimming pools in the D.C. area was located there, so when he and the other boys weren't guarding prisoners of war, they swam and played around in the pool. They felt like they were at a country club, and that's what they called the place.

No one stationed at the prison could tell anyone where he worked -- not even spouses could know. One officer had been working there a couple of years, his wife having no idea of where he went every morning, until he let slip a comment about a swimming pool. "Oh, you're at Fort Hunt," his wife exclaimed, naming exactly the location of P.O. Box 1142. Her stunned husband just stared at her. She was a native of the area and knew where the few swimming pools were. Her husband was shocked that his secret was out, but his wife never told anyone about it. She, like all Americans, was warned constantly not to disclose any information that could help the enemy. "Loose lips may sink ships," was the warning on one of the war posters that were plastered all over the U.S.

Presumably the German soldiers and sailors at P.O. Box 1142 could not have been more dissatisfied with their situation. They not only had suffered the humiliation of being captured by the enemy, but then they had to endure being watched over by teen-aged boys. This is probably the reason they act-ed so arrogantly toward Cooke and the other guards. "If you treat us well, we will take care of you after we win this war," one prisoner told Cooke. These superior-minded prisoners gave Cooke and the other guards copies of their official military I.D. photos to remember them by.

Top intelligence officers at P.O. Box 1142 had trained at the Camp Ritchie Military Intelligence Training Camp in Cascade, Maryland. To be known as a "Ritchie Boy" meant you had been trained to be the best when it came to in-terrogation. Ritchie Boys immersed themselves in their prisoners' language and culture and never used physical force. They used various ploys to get information, like causing arguments between prisoners of different ranks and between prisoners who blamed each other for being captured.

Most of the interrogators were German-trained scientists who had immi-grated to the U.S. and then been drafted into the Army for the specific pur-pose of interrogating German prisoners. Many of them were Jewish and had fled Germany as the Nazis began brutalizing Jewish people. As Germans, they could put the prisoners at ease, speaking their language, talking about home and understanding their culture. They could explain how life was bet-ter in the U.S. and try to convince prisoners to take up the Allied cause.

Cooke's favorite intelligence technique was a simple one. When prison-ers absolutely refused to talk, the intelligence officers would take them out on the town, dressing the prisoners in U.S. officer's uniforms. They took them to eat, drink and do *whatever* they wanted. Invariably, the prisoners would relax and start talking. The U.S. officers, who would only pretend to drink, could get their information and send it to the Pentagon.

During Cooke's assignment at P.O. Box 1142, most of the prisoners had been captured from German submarines – U-boats. At this time, early in the war, the Germans had a heavy presence of U-boats in the Atlantic, blocking

Allied shipping lanes and cutting England off from the U.S. The interrogators were particularly interested in questioning the prisoners about U-boat technology and strategy. With the U-boat intelligence gathered at P.O. Box 1142, the Allies were able to blast the German U-boats out of most of the key Atlantic sea passes.

Sergeant Cooke's story continues in Chapter 21.

The USS Truxtun. Photo courtesy of the U.S. Navy.

3

The USS Truxtun and USS Pollux Tragedy And the Service of Carpenter's Mate Joseph E. Vendola, U.S. Navy

In September of 1940, more than a year before the U.S. entered the war, President Roosevelt announced a "Bases for Destroyers" plan with England as a part of the U.S. national defense program. The U.S. would give England sixty old warships and, in exchange, England, which was getting blasted by Germany, would allow the U.S. to build military bases on land that England controlled in the northern Atlantic Ocean and the Caribbean Sea. Lord Lothian, England's Ambassador to the U.S., had been urging the U.S. to help England, once writing that the British Navy was "strung out terribly thin." The deal would be a great help to England.

Hitler reportedly was furious about the Bases for Destroyers deal. He had been counting on Britain's severe shortage of destroyers, particularly in the northern Atlantic. The all-important Battle of the Atlantic was being waged there, and Germany's U-boats were overwhelming the English and cutting off England's shipping lanes. Germany was advancing through Europe, and England would be entirely isolated if it could not get ships in through the Atlantic.

Most Americans, on the other hand, were happy with the Bases for Destroyers deal, taking comfort in the idea of protecting their homeland from the North and the South. English sailors were more than welcome to take the old destroyers – most Americans did not want their boys on these or any other warships.

Roosevelt had brokered the Bases for Destroyers deal with British Prime

Minister Winston Churchill at a meeting held in Newfoundland, a northern Atlantic island with an important location – the part of North America closest to Europe. Under the deal, the U.S. would build naval, air and army bases on the island. The U.S. would also build bases on Caribbean islands controlled by England.

Before the war, the people of Newfoundland mostly worked as fishermen or farmers, and during the long, northern winters, they struggled with the brutal weather. Roads were very rudimentary, so the little towns and villages where people lived were isolated from one another. Life was so simple that many people did not even use money. A fisherman, for instance, would take his catch of cod and clean and dry it on the wide, flat beaches along the ocean bays. He most likely would then trade his fish at the local market for store credit. Most of the 300,000 or so people in Newfoundland farmed or fished in this way. Others worked in silver mines or paper mills owned by foreign investors. Newfoundland had enjoyed a proud history before the Great Depression as one of Britain's oldest colonies, eventually achieving democratic, self-rule as a British dominion.

The worldwide Great Depression had dealt Newfoundland a devastating blow, however. The government could not repay its World War I debt; foreign investment on the island dropped; and the price of fish plummeted. Almost one third of Newfoundlanders needed some kind of welfare, and the local government did not have money to support them. Public health measures went underfunded, malnutrition was widespread, and diseases such as tuberculosis swept across the island. People pleaded and protested for change.

In debt and desperation, Newfoundland appealed to England for assistance. England agreed to help Newfoundland out of its economic mess, but it exacted a terrible toll from the people of the island. England took back control of Newfoundland. Newfoundlanders lost the right to self-govern. They lost the right to vote. England sent bureaucrats to dictate over the humiliated people of Newfoundland as if they were children. Newfoundland's luck changed, however, thanks to the Bases for Destroyers deal. Money poured into the island, and Newfoundland was transformed.

In early 1941, before the U.S. entered the war, two U.S. military ships quietly departed for Newfoundland, churning through icy waters in the frigid, northern Atlantic winter. They docked in a bay near the tiny town of Argentia, Newfoundland, during a storm, waited for the weather to clear, and the next day, about a thousand U.S. soldiers, sailors and marines stepped onto the windswept island. Under the Bases for Destroyers Program, World War II had come to Newfoundland. Newfoundland, like most of the rest of the world, would never be the same.

The troops who landed in Newfoundland were mostly boys, new to the military. They had grown up during the Depression, had not had much adventure in their lives and were excited to be dressed in their new uniforms and to be on foreign soil. They walked into the town of St. John's and were happy to see that the people there were friendly and welcoming, coming out on the streets to greet them and waving little paper American flags. The next day, about two and a half feet of snow fell, and the troops got a good idea of what was in store for them, weather-wise.

The troops' first task was to build a barracks in the town of Argentia. In the meantime, they lived aboard their ships, docked in the bay. Men and women from across Newfoundland streamed into the area to find work in helping with the construction and with related jobs. Reeling from the worldwide Great Depression, they were thrilled to have employment. They rented rooms in people's homes, and when there were no more beds to rent, they slept on fishing boats docked in the bays.

Once the barracks were completed, the troops and the locals began building the enormous Argentia Base, which included a naval air station in the northern part of Argentia Harbor and an army base in the south. By April 1, 1941, eight months before Pearl Harbor, the base was officially established.

The troops and the locals worked together building U.S. bases, and they played together too. Sports and dances were popular, both on the base and in town at social clubs like the Knights of Columbus. Watching American movies at the base, hearing the troops' music on military radio and trying American food at base parties were all new experiences for the Newfoundlanders. The servicemen enjoyed the food and customs of Newfoundland too, though not the cold, harsh climate. Hundreds of U.S. servicemen married the women they met at dances and parties in Newfoundland.

One occasion in which Americans and Newfoundlanders came together was truly extraordinary. Sailors with the U.S. Navy suffered a tragic accident off the coast of Newfoundland, three months after Pearl Harbor, in February of 1942. The U.S. had been in Newfoundland just over a year. In one of the worst maritime accidents in the war, three U.S. ships went aground in the icy sea off the eastern part of the island. What followed were grievous losses of human life and stunning acts of bravery and humanity. The Herculean efforts of the residents of two small mining villages in Newfoundland to save the men have been much celebrated in the years since, and the U.S. government has described those Newfoundlanders as exemplifying the "inherent courage of mankind."

Joe Vendola was aboard one of those ships. He had enlisted in the U.S. Navy in early 1940 at age nineteen, before the U.S. entered the war. The Great Depression had hit his family hard, so he joined the Navy because he needed a job. He married his wife Regina just before he left for Newfoundland, and six weeks later, he found himself near to death in a frigid winter cyclone just outside of the small town of Lawn, in eastern Newfoundland. Newfoundlanders saved his life.

Vendola was headed to Argentia on the *USS Truxtun*, a destroyer, on the fateful, February night. He had boarded the ship in the Boston Navy Yard, where the ship regularly went for repairs. Aboard ship, Vendola spent his time working his shift as a carpenter and performing watch duty, on the lookout for enemy ships. When he wasn't working, he watched movies, wrote letters home, and attended Catholic mass in the chapel. The men aboard also had access to a hospital, classroom and rec room, but on deck it was all business – machine guns, torpedo launchers and other armaments covered almost every inch of the deck.

The *Truxtun* travelled in convoy, to protect ships that were delivering troops or supplies to various bases, but being in convoy was not much protection from the German "wolf packs." The wolf packs were groups of U-boats stationed in the British shipping lanes, far enough into the Atlantic Ocean that it was difficult for aircraft to reach them and take them out. The Germans would spot the enemy convoys during the day, and then at night, packs of eight or nine submarines would attack the targeted convoy, the same way wolves attack their prey. Many Allied ships were overwhelmed and lost in these attacks and never recovered. The Atlantic Ocean was a vast and deadly area.

Vendola and the others knew their lives were at risk from the weather as well as from the Germans. Some of the deadliest winter storms in North America occur in the frigid, northern Atlantic near Newfoundland. On February 18, 1942, Vendola's convoy was met with a ferocious winter cyclone.

The *USS Pollux* was a freighter carrying bombs, aircraft engines, radio equipment and other supplies for the bases in Argentia. The *Truxtun* and another destroyer, the *USS Wilkes*, escorted the *Pollux*. One of the Navy's newest destroyers, the state-of-the-art *Wilkes* was the flagship and led the convoy, following a ziz-zag pattern to avoid detection by the enemy. Vendola was still learning the ropes aboard ship. He was told that the convoy was maintaining radio silence to avoid detection. He did not need to be told that when they hit the blinding snow storm, the ships' crews had trouble seeing each other.

With the *Wilkes* leading the way, just a few hours away from Argentia, all three ships came too close to shore during the storm, due to navigational problems. At around 4:00 a.m. on February 18, the three ships ran aground in the rocky water off the southern coast, within minutes of each other. The *Wilkes* managed to free itself, and its crew could see the *Pollux* impaled on a boulder but could not get close enough to help. The crews on the *Truxtun* and *Pollux* did not know what was going on with the rest of the convoy. Vendola was in his bunk, sleeping, when the ship started shaking and making a horrible noise. He and his bunkmates thought that the ship had been torpedoed by German U-boats. Vendola and the others ran up to the deck of the ship.

Vendola and his crewmates faced unbelievable conditions and almost certain death. In the darkness of the dead of night, in a blinding snowstorm with gale force winds, they were aboard a ship that was trapped by the rocks on the ocean floor. The deck and equipment were covered in ice. Waves crashed around, as tall as twelve feet high, and every so often the icy waves crashed across the deck. The fellow next to Vendola was picked up by a wave and smashed to death. The men could hear grinding steel and knew that the ship was going to break apart and sink. The ship's bow had hit the rocks, so she was tilted forward. Bodies floated past Vendola toward the ship's stern and down into the water.

The *Truxtun* was not far from shore. Vendola couldn't believe it, but as dawn broke, they could see that they were only about forty-five feet from land. Reaching land, however, did not mean salvation. The ship had gone aground in Chamber's Cove. The shore there consisted of a narrow icy beach enclosed by sheer, ice-covered cliffs that towered over three-hundred-feet high. At the top of the cliffs, in the snow, only a long wooden fence and a small shed could be seen. Vendola noticed that most of the crew had come onto deck. They formulated a plan: get to shore, somehow scale the cliff, and then follow the fence to find help.

In the morning's light, the exhausted sailors who had survived to this point tried various means of getting to shore. Men in wooden lifeboats were lowered into the raging waters, only to have the boats smash into the sides of the ship, dropping the sailors into the waves. The ship was spewing oil, and everyone became covered in it. Many men suffocated in the slime. Eventually about twenty survivors made it to shore, soaked to the skin. The lifelines and rubber rafts they had used to get there were entangled in the rocks and rendered useless, leaving about one hundred sailors on the rocking, sinking ship, soaking wet and clinging to the ship's frigid steel rails.

Rock climbing is a tough pursuit, requiring special equipment and hours of practice. That Ash Wednesday morning in Chamber's Cove, two crew members from the *Truxtun*, Edward Bergeron and Edward Petterson, exhausted, freezing cold and soaking wet, gave themselves a rock climbing lesson in a blinding snowstorm. They had knives and rope for equipment. Amazingly, they scaled the entire 300 feet of the sheer, soaring, icy cliff. At the top though, there was disappointment. The men could detect no signs of life around them other than the fence and the shed, just snow as far as the eye could see. Petterson collapsed on some hay in the otherwise empty shed, and Bergeron, taking a wild guess as to which direction to head toward, set out walking along the fence to find help. The storm raged on.

After a three-mile hike, Bergeron came to the mining town of St. Lawrence, appearing in the sleet almost as an apparition and, near to collapsing, told his mind-boggling story. The mine halted its operations. The entire town of about one thousand people rallied together for a massive rescue effort. The miners hiked through the snowstorm to the tops of the cliffs with sleds and equipment. When attempts to haul the men up failed – because they were too weak to hold on to ropes – the miners bravely lowered themselves down the icy cliffs and hauled up each survivor, one by one.

Hours after the ordeal began, more than a hundred men were still in the water, having somehow survived the elements. They clung to what was left of the ship as it broke apart. Giant waves crashed over them and swept men onto the rocks to die. With utmost heroism, the miners went into the frigid water, on the rocks, in the sleet, with the windswept waves washing over them, and carried men to shore. They rescued as many as they could. They made the men fires and gave them the clothes off their backs. Then they hauled them up the cliffs, one by one. The women of the town bathed and nursed the men in their own homes throughout the day and night. All the townspeople took clothes, food and supplies from their homes to give to the sailors.

Vendola was conscious when he was dragged up the cliff. He passed out once he made it to the top. When he came to, he found himself with no clothes on, in a strange kitchen, being bathed by a kind woman.

In the meanwhile, the men on the *Pollux* were in the same horrific situation a few miles away in the water at Lawn Point. Townspeople discovered the tragic scene late in the afternoon on Ash Wednesday. The residents of the nearby town of Lawn and people from St. Lawrence carried out another heroic rescue mission to save whom they could. Of the 389 souls aboard the two ships, 203 died. The men whose lives were saved would never forget their ordeal. For one crewmember, however, the experience was truly life changing.

Lanier Phillips was aboard the *Truxtun* that day. Phillips was an African-American man, the great-grandson of a slave, who had grown up in segregated Georgia before enlisting in the segregated U.S. Navy. All branches of the U.S. Armed Forces were segregated during World War II, and blacks and other minorities were generally given menial work, no matter their education, intelligence or skills. The military reflected the culture of the U.S. at the time.

As a black man, Phillips was assigned to serve as a mess attendant, doing work similar to that of a waiter or butler. He realized when he enlisted that his opportunities in the Navy would be limited because of his race, but he decided that life would be better there than at home in Georgia. The Ku Klux Klan, an organization that promotes racism, held official, formal parades though his town, and Klansmen rampaged the black neighborhoods for sport. The Klan burned down the only school for black children in his town, and parents wondered whether their children would ever be educated. Phillips was taught never to look a white person in the eye because he could be lynched if he seemed insubordinate. At the time the *Truxton* ran aground, Phillips had served about fifteen months in the segregated Navy, and the fear, mistrust and hatred of white people ingrained in him in Georgia still dominated his world view.

In responding to the shipwreck, much to Phillips' awe and disbelief, the good people of Lawn and St. Lawrence treated him exactly as they treated the white men whose lives they were trying to save. The miners made the same heroic efforts to bring him to safety as they did the others, and the women nursed him back to health with the same loving care that they showed the white men. A miner's wife named Violet Pike brought him to her home, wrapped him in woolen blankets and fed him warm broth in front of her kitchen fire all night long.

Of the four black men aboard the *Truxtun*, Phillips was the only survivor. It was customary for black crewmembers in the Navy to be told not to leave their ships in foreign countries – they often thought they would be lynched if they did – so perhaps the other black men aboard the *Truxtun* were afraid to leave the ship, or perhaps they just could not survive the brutal elements. Of course there was no chance that the black crew members would be lynched at Chamber's Cove. Newfoundlanders had not been taught to be racist, and the rescuers had probably never seen a black person before. At first they thought that Phillips' skin was dark from the oil in the water.

During peacetime, survivors of such a tragedy would be given much needed time to recuperate, but this was war. A couple days after the shipwrecks, a U.S. Navy ship picked up the survivors, brought them back home to the U.S. and redeployed them. Vendola served aboard the *USS Wyoming*, a training ship for gunners that operated in the Chesapeake Bay, and the *USS Florence Nightingale*, which carried troops, equipment and prisoners of war in the Pacific Theater and earned four battle stars. Vendola and the other survivors had to move right along from the tragedy, like so many others who suffered horrors in the war. In fact, Vendola did not learn much of the details about the tragedy in Chamber's Cove until after he returned home from the war.

Carpenter's Mate Vendola's story concludes in Chapter 24.

A line-up of B-25 Mitchel medium bombers on the deck of the USS Hornet in preparation for the Doolittle Raid over Japan in 1942.
Photo courtesy of the U.S. Naval Historical Center.

4

Japan

Japan has few natural resources and intended to build an empire in the Pacific, in part to have easy access to oil, food and other necessities, but also as a matter of ethnic pride. Many Japanese people felt that their country was taking its rightful place in the world as a territorial leader, like the U.S. and Britain. Japanese patriotism was fierce, its citizens having been taught that their emperor was a deity to be worshipped. Even the emperor's name was sacred and not to be uttered. Some Japanese military troops were overly zealous about fighting for their country. Others were bitter about the racism they perceived from the West. These men committed atrocities in the places that Japan invaded.

Japan invaded the Chinese province of Manchuria in 1931. The League of Nations asked Japan to withdraw from Manchuria, but it refused to do so. In 1932, Japan invaded the Chinese city of Shanghai. Finally, in 1937, Japan launched a full-scale invasion of China, starting near Beijing. In December of that year, the Japanese carried out a seven-week-long terror raid on the Chinese Nationalist capital of Nanking, in what is known as The Rape of Nanking. During this time, the Japanese raped, murdered and brutalized hundreds of thousands of Chinese civilians. It was a reign of terror. China suffered terribly until the Allies defeated Japan in 1945. More than fifteen million Chinese people would die during World War II, an almost unfathomable number of deaths.

The U.S. had been urging Japan to retreat from China since the invasion of Manchuria and during the years leading up to Pearl Harbor, finally began restricting U.S. exports of oil and other commodities to Japan. Japan sorely needed these commodities. As a part of the operation in which it attacked the U.S. at Pearl Harbor, Japan also attacked Guam, the Philippines, Wake Island, Hong Kong, and the Malay Peninsula. Japan hit hard in the Pacific.

The people of the attacked countries endured horrific treatment as the Japanese took control over them. Some of the Japanese troops raped, murdered, tortured and committed mass executions of the innocent Pacific Islanders.

The U.S. and its allies began fighting the Japanese immediately after Pearl Harbor but would battle for months and suffer terribly before seeing much success. U.S. morale at home was low. Many American lives were being lost and people wondered whether the U.S. could beat Japan.

In the spring of 1942, the U.S. launched an attack on the Japanese homeland, headed by the legendary Lt. Colonel James H. Doolittle. On April 18, 1942, the USS Hornet headed toward Japan with sixteen B-25 medium bombers. Their mission was to bomb munitions centers in Japan and then head to China, to land in friendly airbases. A Japanese patrol boat spotted the Hornet on its way to Japan, so the U.S. changed the mission in case the Japanese were expecting them. With the mission altered, the B-25s ran low on fuel after successfully hitting their targets. Many crewmen heroically bailed out at sea or crashed down in China. The Chinese helped rescue those they could. The Doolittle Tokyo Raiders were some of the first heroes of World War II.

Later in 1942, in August, the U.S launched its first major offensive against the Japanese on the island of Guadalcanal. Americans started to feel more encouraged about the War in the Pacific.

At around the same time that the American public heard about the heroic Doolittle Raid, one of the most horrific episodes in the War in the Pacific occurred: the Bataan Death March. Right after Pearl Harbor, the Japanese attacked the island of Luzon in the Philippines, taking out two-thirds of the U.S. Army Air Force fleet and destroying its airfields. U.S. and Filipino troops, about 100,000 in all, retreated to the Bataan Peninsula and tried to fight off the Japanese there for months, but the Allies were poorly equipped and lacked adequate food or medicine. They suffered from malaria and subsisted on as little as 800 calories a day. Many of them were airmen and had not been trained for ground fighting.

In April, the Japanese finally overpowered the Allies and the Bataan

Death March began, with brutal Japanese soldiers marching the weak and sick American and Filipino prisoners sixty-five miles up the east coast of Bataan to a prison camp. The guards committed horrific acts of torture on the prisoners all along the way. More than 10,000 prisoners died in the march, and many others died on "hell ships" used to transport prisoners to work as slave laborers. News of the Bataan Death March did not emerge until months later, after a prison escape.

The Allies finally turned the tide against Japan in June of 1942, in the Battle of Midway. After the Doolittle Raid, in order to prevent another attack on its homeland, Japan planned to launch a huge attack on the Midway Atoll, where the U.S. and its allies had a base. The Allies, however, learned about the plan ahead of time, by decoding secret Japanese messages.

When the Japanese arrived at Midway, Admiral Chester W. Nimitz, Commander of the U.S. Pacific Fleet, had the area completely armed, on land, at sea and in the air. The U.S. was waiting with guns a-blazing, and it completely overpowered the enemy. Japan lost an enormous amount of air and naval equipment in the battle – it was the biggest defeat Japan had suffered in more than a century in terms of equipment and lives lost. Defeating Japan at the Midway Atoll was the first major success for the Allies; it turned the tide of the War in the Pacific in the Allies' favor, but Japan remained strong, and the Allies still had a lot of work ahead of them.

This poster appeared at First and Front Streets in the part of San Francisco from which Japanese-Americans were first removed.
Photo courtesy of the U.S. National Archives, number 536017.

Photograph of a Japanese internment camp in Manzanar, California, taken during a dust storm by Dorothea Lange on July 3, 1942.
Photo courtesy of the U.S. National Archives, number 210-G-10C-839.

The Fate of Japanese-Americans During the War

Throughout the decades leading up to the war, more than a quarter mil-lion Japanese had immigrated to the U.S., living mainly on the West Coast and in Hawaii, where they generally farmed and operated small businesses. For the most part, Japanese-Americans enjoyed financial success. They also endured racism. After the Japanese attack on Pearl Harbor, people urged Congress to remove Japanese-Americans from the West Coast, arguing that they could operate as spies for Japan. The notion of the United States round-ing up an ethnic group consisting of law-abiding U.S. citizens and legal res-idents and jailing them is mind-boggling – but it happened.

In March of 1942, the U.S. Army declared the West Coast a military zone and asked all Japanese-Americans to volunteer to leave their homes, farms and businesses and move to internment camps. Those who did not volunteer were forcibly taken to the camps, which were located in isolated areas in sev-eral western states. The camps looked like prisons and were fenced-in and guarded. More than 120,000 Japanese-Americans were imprisoned in these camps, and most of them lost all they had financially.

Seventy thousand of these prisoners were U.S. citizens, and some were drafted into the military. Others enlisted, going off to fight while their fami-lies lived at the camps. Japanese-American troops, who were segregated in the military, visited their families at the camp while on leaves from service. More than 30,000 Japanese-Americans served in the war.

Hitler's Nazi troops marching through Warsaw, Poland, in September of 1939. Photo courtesy of the U.S. National Archives, number 200-SFF-52.

5

Germany

Germany in the years leading up to World War II was in economic shambles. Inflation was so high that German currency was virtually worthless. People used money as wallpaper. Those who still had jobs would get their pay and run to the stores to buy food before the prices rose yet again. At desperate times like these, charismatic individuals who can convince people that they can solve their problems may rise to power regardless of their political platform. Adolf Hitler joined the socialist Nazi Party in the 1920's, took it over, and transformed it into an Aryan white-supremacist organization. By early 1933, he took power as Chancellor of Germany. Within months Hitler's paramilitary police force, the SS, began brutalizing and overtaking local German governmental offices; he opened the first of what would be dozens of concentration camps and sub-camps; and he instituted the first boycott of Jewish businesses.

Hitler believed the ethnic German Aryans were a superior "race" of human beings and as such were entitled to a large territory of European land, which they would take by force from what he considered to be inferior races, such as the Slavs and the Poles. When Hitler's forces invaded Poland in 1939, marking the start of the war in Europe, they arrested thousands of religious, intellectual and community leaders in Poland and killed them. They forced more than one million Poles from their homes – and left them without shelter to starve or freeze to death -- to make room for Germans. Hitler planned to abolish all but the most rudimentary of education in Poland and reduce

Poland to a slave nation in service to the Germans. The plan in Poland was what Hitler had in mind for most of Europe, with the exception of the Jewish people.

While it is widely believed that Hitler found Jewish people to be another inferior race, an alternative school of thought is that Hitler saw Jewish people not as inferior but as a threat. Hitler realized that the religious teachings of Judaism contradicted and thus threatened the basic notion he was promoting, that some "races," such as Germans, were superior. He also believed that Jewish people, many of whom were prominent in Germany, would try to undermine the Nazi efforts and might be successful in doing so. Step by step, beginning with boycotts, racist propaganda and institutionalized mistreatment of Jewish people, Hitler's Nazi Party eventually formed a plan to systematically murder each and every Jewish person in Europe. Tragically, he was hugely successful.

Throughout the war, Jewish people from twenty European countries were executed by military units or were taken to concentration and labor camps where they were shot; others were starved, mistreated and tortured at camps until they died; others were shipped to death camps, which had been built to carry out mass executions of Jewish people. At these killing factories, Jewish men, women and children were marched into airtight chambers and murdered with poisonous gas. The percentage of the Jewish population slaughtered in the Holocaust is estimated to have been as follows: in Poland, 91% of the Jewish population was killed; in Greece, 87%; in Lithuania, 85%; in Romania, 84%; in Latvia, 84%; in Slovakia, 80%; in Hungary, 74%; in the Netherlands, 71%; in Bohemia Moravia, 60%; in Luxembourg, 55%; in Belgium, 45%; in Norway, 45%; in Estonia, 44%; in the USSR, 36%; in Germany, 36%; in Austria, 35%; in France, 22%; and in smaller percentages in other countries. Hitler and his forces were responsible for the deaths of approximately six million Jewish people during the war.

The atrocities committed by the Nazis during the war cannot be overstated. In addition to decimating the European Jewish population, the Germans systematically killed gay people and a group of Europeans with Indian heritage who were known as Roma or Gypsies; they systematically killed sick and disabled people; they systematically performed forced abortions upon women deemed to have genetic disorders; they systematically performed unspeakable, sadistic medical procedures upon prisoners, stole children from parents to become Nazi youth or prisoners in camps, and had female prisoners serve as sex slaves for military officials.

The Allied Powers plan for D-Day at the Conference of Yalta in February of 1945. From left, seated, are British Prime Minister Winston Churchill, U.S. President Franklin Roosevelt and Soviet Premier Josef Stalin.
Photo courtesy of the U.S. National Archives, number 111-SC-260486.

6

The First Infantry
And the Service of Sergeant Milton L. Krom,
U.S. Army

The infantry are the foot soldiers, the men who fight on the ground. Carrying guns and heavy packs of equipment, they walk through war zones amidst bombs, mines, gunfire and more. They witness the horrors of war closely and personally. Milton L. Krom served as a sergeant, trucking ammunition to soldiers on the battlefields, in the 32nd Field Artillery Regiment of the 1st Infantry Division of the U.S. Army.

The 1st Infantry Division is legendary -- its World War II experiences have been portrayed in books and movies. It was established during World War I and is nicknamed "the Big Red One" because its arm badge features the number "1" in red. It was the first U.S. division to fight in Europe and Africa during World War II and quickly became the most hardened and experienced group of U.S. soldiers in Europe.

Krom, age ninety-six, descends from a long line of American patriots, so while growing up, he had no doubt in his mind that he would serve his country one day. His great-grandfather fought in the American Revolutionary War and the War of 1812. Krom's second wife Marie likes to point out that this family fought for their country before it *was* a country. Krom's grandfather was a Union soldier in the American Civil War. Krom, who is a member of the Sons of the American Revolutionary War, explains that his father did not serve in the military because of a physical disability; he had only one eye.

Krom was a senior in high school during the 1939-1940 school year. The world was at war, and the national defense program was well underway. Talk of war was everywhere. Once he graduated from high school, Krom married his sweetheart, Rose, and enlisted in the Army on June 26, 1940 because he followed the news and was fairly certain that the U.S. would have to fight. Krom was assigned to the 1st Infantry, one of the four divisions that had remained on active duty during the peacetime following World War I. After basic training, he was assigned to the artillery and was given the choice of taking artillery training in Vermont or in Texas. Krom was surprised and pleased to be given a choice. He opted for Vermont because he and Rose had decided that she would live in New York City to be near family, while he served.

Krom trained for well over a year, practicing maneuvers and aquatic landings in North Carolina after his stint in Vermont. By this point, the U.S. had entered the war. Sometimes Rose visited her husband, renting a room near his base. He would get a weekend pass, and they could spend a couple of days together. After Rose gave birth to their first child, a son, Krom saw his wife and new baby on furloughs. He travelled to New York, and he and Rose could have a few days of being husband and wife and enjoying their new baby together. During the springtime of 1942, Krom was sent for final training at the enormous Indiantown Gap Military Reservation in Pennsylvania. On June 21st, 1942, his unit was told to prepare to go overseas.

When Rose learned of her husband's deployment, she went to church, lit a candle and prayed for him. After that, she prayed for him every day during the war.

On August 2, 1942, Krom shipped out on the *RMS Queen Mary*, an English luxury liner built for 5,000 passengers. During the war it served as a troop carrier, and on a typical voyage like Krom's, about 20,000 troops would cram onto the ship, sleeping all over the place. Even the beautiful swimming pool had been drained so cots could be set up inside it. The voyage was very dangerous because this early in the war, large numbers of German U-boats patrolled the Atlantic Ocean. The ship had no escort and travelled in a zigzag path to avoid detection.

The zigzagging was a slow process, so it took several days to cross over. Some of the boys were nervous. Others were excited and anxious to get over there and take out the enemy. Only several months had passed since Pearl Harbor, and these boys were some of the first to go off to fight. They landed in Scotland on August 7 and then went immediately by rail to Tidworth Barracks in England for more training.

The 1st Infantry was preparing for Operation Torch, a very ambitious amphibious landing in North Africa. Securing North Africa was important for many reasons – chiefly, it enabled the Allies to establish a shipping base in the Mediterranean area, and it pushed the Axis Powers back from a strategic location.

The Axis Powers in Europe – Germans, Italians and the German-backed Vichy French – controlled a strip of North Africa between Tunisia and Egypt and had about 100,000 troops stationed in the area. The Allies stormed the coast with more than 100,000 troops on November 8, 1942, in three landing spots: Casablanca, Oran and Algiers. The just-completed World War II movie *Casablanca* was rushed into movie theaters in the U.S. a few weeks after this operation.

Krom landed in Oran. The fighting was long and intense with advances and retreats, and Krom and his buddies fought all the way through Bizerte and Tunisia, after which the Germans and Italians surrendered, six long months later, on May 12, 1943.

Prior to this operation, some British leaders reportedly had expressed concerns that the U.S. troops were green – they had never seen battle. Indeed, like Krom, most of the troops of the 1st Infantry who arrived in Africa were average young American men, boys really, and had not been soldiers before the war. Crossing the line from citizen to soldier is a tremendous transformation. Taking human life is a part of the soldier's duty to his country and to his fellow soldiers, and it is the soldier's cross to bear.

Very few if any of these young men, quite likely, had ever seriously risked their lives, taken a life or seen their buddies die, as they would now. They were far from their homes, on desert land, taking up guns against other young men who didn't look much different from themselves. They were not fighting a natural enemy: the U.S. had been strongly isolationist until Pearl Harbor, when it was attacked by Japan, not by Italy or Germany, whose Nazi atrocities were not yet widely known. Some of the American soldiers were of German descent, fighting against German soldiers.

Like most of his fellow soldiers of the 1st Infantry, Krom arrived in Africa a novice and left a seasoned veteran. The U.S. endured brutal combat against the Germans in the Battle of Kasserine Pass, suffered heavy losses of life and did not win the battle. Soon thereafter, General George Patton took command of the 3rd Army, which included the 1st Infantry, and led the U.S.

to a hard-won victory at the Battle of El Guettar in March of 1943. Patton reportedly told his troops in North Africa, "We shall attack and attack until we are exhausted, and then we shall attack again."

Krom was truly a soldier now. Back at home in New York, his wife Rose gave birth to their second son.

At one point while fighting each other in Africa, the Americans and Germans took a break to bury their dead. Krom was fighting the Germans, but he felt that the German and American boys were together in a lot of ways. During their small truce, Krom helped bury his dead friends, while across the battlefront, the Germans did the same for their own. Maintaining one's humanity on the battlefield in ways like this is essential to recovering, possibly, from the psychological wounds of combat. These young men not only witnessed but also had to contribute to unspeakable human suffering. That is the duty of the soldier.

The 1st Infantry emerged from the fierce warfare in Africa as a tight-knit, battle-scarred and thoroughly experienced group. Their legend was growing. The next Allied effort was to liberate Sicily, an Italian island located in the Mediterranean, two miles from the "toe" of Italy. Patton commanded the U.S. forces in this and reportedly announced that he would not undertake the operation without the 1st Infantry.

On July 9, 1943, just two months after securing North Africa, the Allies invaded Sicily, in Operation Husky. Although not as widely known as the Normandy Invasion on D-Day, this operation covered the largest landing zone and landed the most initial troops of any amphibious operation during the war. Over half a million Allied troops fought in the five-week-long battle, which toppled Benito Mussolini's dictatorship over Italy, led to the Allied victory there and for Hitler opened a critical vulnerability in southern Europe.

Krom and his buddies fought the Germans and Italians in Sicily. After they liberated Sicily, they returned to England. Many of the men went into the hospital there, injured or sick with malaria or other diseases. Krom was hospitalized with malaria. Some men had "shell shock," having gone mad from the combat. Most of the men with shell shock were silent and unresponsive to other people.

After the men were treated in the hospital, those who had recovered began to prepare for D-Day. Krom didn't know if it was going to be successful – it felt like a gamble to him, but a gamble they had to take. Although the exact date was not decided until the last moment, and therefore was unknown to almost everyone, D-Day, the "designated day," would be June 6, 1944. On this day, the Allied Powers, led by the U.S. and Britain, would land on the very dangerous beaches of Normandy, France, which was under German control and heavily defended, and begin a massive invasion of German-occupied Europe. Although the Axis powers had been severely weakened by their losses in Africa and Italy, most people felt that there was no choice but for the D-Day invasion to succeed if they were to free Europe – and save the world – from Hitler's oppression. Krom thought that D-Day was crucial. He and many others thought that the Germans and Japanese seemed to have a grip on the entire world.

Sergeant Krom's story continues in Chapter 12.

Recruiting poster by Steele Savage.
Photo courtesy of the U.S. National Archives, number 44-PA-820.

The U.S. Army Air Forces Nurse Corps and the Service of Captain Lois Crook

During the 1920's and the Great Depression, the people of North Dakota, a farming state, seemed to suffer more than the farmers across the rest of the country. In most of the U.S., farmers at least had food, but that wasn't always the case in North Dakota. Dust Bowl storms swept through the state, wiping away the topsoil used for planting. Many farmers went years without decent crops, and their livestock were thin and sickly. Cows and hens could no longer produce milk and eggs. Some farmers tried to move to cities like Fargo, but there were few jobs, and they paid very little. Tens of thousands of people moved out of the state and tried their luck elsewhere. People in these other states posted signs telling newcomers to turn back.

In some parts of the North Dakota, adults and children were emaciated from hunger. Living for years with no money to spend, people's clothes turned to rags. Houses were repaired with scraps of wood and tin. Without adequate fuel, clothing, or the means to keep their houses insulated, people endured bitterly cold winters in poorly heated homes.

Lois Eileen Storhaug, now Lois Crook , was born on April 4, 1922, in Lisbon, North Dakota. While conditions where Crook lived were not as harsh as they were in much of the state, times were very tough. To this day, more than seventy years later, Crook vividly remembers the cold and the hopelessness of those years. She's never been able to watch television footage of the Great Depression or the Dust Bowl.

Crook's treasured possession as a child was a book she received one

Christmas: The Book of Knowledge, an encyclopedia for children. It was a part of a series of books, but she had only the one. Crook loved to learn and pored over the book's text, pictures and illustrations. She was an honors student all throughout grade school and high school. In 1939, Crook graduated as one of the top two students in her class and would have loved to go on to a four-year college, but of course there was no money for that.

The Trinity Hospital School of Nursing had a three-year program, which Crook could attend for free in exchange for working at the hospital. Becoming a nurse was not Crook's first choice, but it was a way for this intelligent young lady to make something of her life. After nursing school, Crook was recruited to serve in the Army during the war as a nurse, and her service in the war would transform her life forever.

Crook was in her last year of nursing school on December 7, 1941, working a half-day in the hospital wards because it was a Sunday. Radios were few and far between in the poor, rural state of North Dakota, but news of the attack on Pearl Harbor soon reached the hospital. Many young men – doctors, patients and staff – immediately announced that they were going to serve in the war. Some boys even jumped into their cars and headed for military recruiting stations – which, they learned, were closed on Sundays. Crook soon realized that her country needed her to serve too.

The Red Cross recruited nurses for the Army and Navy Nurses Corps, and they pursued the new nurses very aggressively. Recruiting posters appeared around the hospital, and the one Crook noticed the most showed a soldier lying wounded on the battlefield, with Uncle Sam pointing his finger at the reader and a caption asking, "What if this were your husband, and no one was there to help him?"

Crook graduated from her nursing program in August of 1943. She then sat for and passed the state exam, becoming a registered nurse. Red Cross recruiters at the state registration office asked to speak with her. Crook was happy to lend her new skills to the war effort, so she enrolled in the Red Cross' military qualification program. Only fifty percent of the program's participants could get admitted for military service, but Crook was brainy and passed the qualification program with flying colors. Crook chose to enlist in the Army Air Forces. The Air Forces seemed kind of glamorous, she thought, because it was just coming into its own as a military branch.

Crook was inducted into the Army Air Forces on January 4, 1944 as a 2nd

Lieutenant. By the end of 1944, more than 6,000 nurses served at Army Air Forces hospitals across the U.S. Several hundred of these nurses volunteered to be flight nurses, evacuating patients from overseas. Coming from such a rural, isolated background, however, Crook found her experiences serving in the U.S. to be foreign enough. She worked at bases in the deserts of the West and Southwest, and, compared with life in North Dakota, she felt like she was in another country.

Crook's first culture shock was learning that the military was segregated and that blacks and other minorities were considered to be inferior. At basic training in Colorado, she noticed that one of the patients did not have a room inside the hospital but instead stayed on the sun porch, day and night. When she asked him if he would like to move inside, he declined without telling her why. It never dawned on Crook that he had to stay on the porch because he was a black man. There was no way to segregate blacks from whites inside the small hospital, so black patients stayed on the porch and were treated for their wounds and illnesses on the porch. Segregation was a part of the culture of the U.S. at this time, and the military reflected that culture.

Crook had been raised well, having been taught to treat people politely and kindly and therefore had many experiences like the sun porch incident. For instance, she found it difficult to get in the habit, as she was now instructed, of not addressing black people with titles of respect, such as "Mr." or "Mrs."

Crook's next culture shock came when she was sent to the Marfa Air Forces Base in Southwest Texas, a small town near the Mexican border where the movie *Giant* had been filmed. She found it exciting to be so close to Mexico, which seemed to be a very foreign country.

Marfa was a sleepy little town until the Army Air Forces took it over, building a base for advanced pilot training with more than 500 training planes and six runways. Crook's job largely was to help treat the victims of plane crashes and mid-air collisions in a temporary, field hospital that had been built on the base. It was a tough job, with only seven or eight nurses assigned to the base. Some of the victims of the accidents did not survive, becoming war casualties before ever earning their pilot's wings.

Crook was next sent to work at a base in Victorville, California, in March of 1944. Before she arrived, a young man trained there who would go on to become one of the most legendary Air Force pilots of all time. In September of 1941, just before Pearl Harbor, Charles ("Chuck") Yeager enlisted in the Army Air Forces in Victorville, as an aircraft mechanic. He was later chosen for flight training, earned his wings, and was deployed to England in November of 1943, as a fighter pilot. The rest of his career, including going on to become the first pilot to break the sound barrier, is a major chapter in aviation and American history.

Crook arrived at an exciting time for the pilot cadets, ground crews, trainers and other personnel. Their work was important and highly technological, and their enormous base had overtaken the little town of Victorville. Women from the Women Airforce Service Pilots or WASP program helped the men train by piloting planes so the cadets could practice navigation and bombardment. Women also served as a part of the Women's Army Auxiliary Corps, the WAACs, but Crook couldn't help feeling that the nurses held a superior position to the WAACs. Nurses were all trained professionals, and they all were officers in the Army Air Forces.

Some of the troops who were from the California area were lucky. Their family or friends could visit them, many of them staying at the Stewart Hotel in the little downtown area of Victorville. Crook's family was too far away to visit her, but she wrote home often and looked forward to the letters she received from friends and family. The folks back home were proud of this smart girl – they had always known that she would go far in life.

Captain Crook's story concludes in Chapter 24.

The Women's Army Auxiliary Corps

After Roosevelt signed the bill that created the Women's Army Auxiliary Corps on May 15, 1942, he appointed Oveta Culp Hobby as Director of the WAAC, with the rank of Colonel. A former business executive and newspaper editor, Colonel Hobby had been Chief of the Women's Interest Section in the Public Relations Bureau of the War Department and had lobbied heavily for the legislation creating the WAAC.

Colonel Hobby addressed the first class of women to train to be officers in the U.S. Army. She spoke eloquently, as the occasion merited: "You have a debt to democracy and a date with destiny." Later, Hobby helped secure the legislation that transformed WAAC from an auxiliary corps into the Women's Army Corps, a part of the regular Army, not an auxiliary. Upon her retirement from the Army in 1945, Hobby was awarded the Distinguished Service Medal.

AMERICANOS TODOS
★
LUCHAMOS POR LA
VICTORIA

★ AMERICANS ALL ★
LET'S FIGHT FOR VICTORY

A 1943 U.S. War Poster by Artist Leon Helguera depicting the Mexican-American contribution to the war effort.
Photo courtesy of the University of North Texas Digital Library.

Latino-Americans in the War

More than one half million Latino-Americans fought in World War II, an estimate because the military for the most part did not segregate Latinos or keep records indicating whether a serviceman or woman was of Latino descent. While many Latinos faced discrimination at home, they served with distinction in the war.

The 65th Infantry Regiment, based in Puerto Rico, had been formed in 1899, after the U.S. took Puerto Rico in the Spanish-American War. Known as The Borinqueneers, in recognition of Puerto Rico's original, indigenous name, the predominantly Puerto Rican 65th served in Panama, North Africa and Europe during the war. They saw combat and served with distinction, but critics say that they were not given much opportunity to perform because of racial bias. The 65th is mostly remembered for its outstanding service in the Korean War and was awarded the Congressional Gold Medal of Honor in 2014.

A highly regarded unit of World War II was the 1st Regimental Combat Team, an Arizona National Guard Unit comprised mainly of Mexican Americans and Native Americans, known as "The Bushmasters," after a deadly snake. They were sent to guard Panama against a potential invasion, and they trained to fight in the jungles there. Their jungle-fighting skills became so well regarded that General MacArthur personally requested that they be assigned to him. The Bushmasters went on to battle throughout the Southwest Pacific Theater and were selected to spearhead the planned invasion of the Japanese mainland in Operation Downfall. It has been widely reported that General MacArthur called the Bushmasters "the greatest fighting command team ever deployed for battle."

The New Mexico National Guard deployed to the Philippines two units of officers and enlisted men, most of whom were Latino and could speak Spanish. They worked well with the Filipino Army because many of them spoke Spanish as well. Many of the troops from New Mexico, along with the Filipinos, endured or died in the Bataan Death March in March of 1943, one of the worst atrocities of the war. The New Mexico National Guard still pays tribute to these heroes.

The first Hispanic to win the Congressional Gold Medal of Honor in World War II was Private Jose P. Martinez, a New Mexico native who was drafted into the 7th Infantry Division. In June of 1942, right after its enormous defeat at Midway, Japan invaded U.S. territory: the Aleutians, a chain of islands more than 1,000 miles long that curves westward from Alaska toward Japan in the northern Pacific Ocean. Six hundred and fifty miles from where the Aleutians end, the Japanese Kuriles Islands begin. Mountainous, snow-covered and usually stormy, the Aleutians were not fit for much military use, but the U.S. could not allow the Japanese to occupy them.

On April 30, 1943, Martinez and other members of the 7th Infantry Division, based in Fort Ord, California, arrived in the Aleutians, staying aboard their crowded troop transport ships in America-occupied territory. They were waiting for storms to clear for their attack on Attu Island, which the Japanese occupied. The unseasoned soldiers would fight in the snow and cold in regular combat gear because of a shortage of cold weather uniforms.

On May 11, members of the 7th Infantry landed on Attu, with little air support due to thick fog. The fighting was brutal. The Americans undertook attacks and then had to cancel them. Some described the Japanese troops as fanatical. On May 15, a U.S. report to headquarters explained that progress in the battle on Attu would be slow, costly and require additional troops. Eleven days later, on May 26, Martinez and other soldiers were bogged down yet again in an attempt to push the Japanese out of their position on a snow-covered mountain pass. The Americans' chances of success seemed grim. American soldiers were trapped under heavy machinegun, rifle and mortar fire, and the men were discouraged. Martinez stood up, however, in the midst of enemy fire. He picked up his rifle and began to fire back. He urged his fellow soldiers to continue to fight and set an example for the others to follow. Martinez fired upon and eliminated five Japanese positions and eventually led troops up more than 150 feet to the pass, to success. There, Martinez collapsed, mortally wounded. The Congressional Gold Medal of Honor Citation for Martinez commends his "conspicuous gallantry and intrepidity above and beyond the call of duty in action with the enemy." The U.S. took back the Aleutian Islands three months after Martinez' heroic leadership, in August of 1943.

Marine PFC Guy Gabaldon, who was Mexican American, was born on March 22, 1926, and grew up in a rough Los Angeles neighborhood during the Great Depression. He would go on to become one of the most fascinating heroes of World War II. Gabaldon was a short kid and to show that he was tough, he got into a lot of trouble, jumping trains and fighting anyone on a dare. In junior high school he met two Japanese-American boys, Lane and Lyle Nakano, and their family, and his friendship with the Nakanos changed the course of his life. He spent a lot of time at the Nakanos' home, often for days on end. He still got into a lot of fights – he said even as an adult that he had always loved a good fight – but he developed a fascination for the Japanese culture and learned some of the language.

Gabaldon was devastated when the Nakanos were sent to live in an internment camp. He dropped out of school, at age sixteen, and in 1943, on his seventeenth birthday, he joined the Marines. At five feet, three inches tall and with a bad ear, Gabaldon didn't quite meet the Marines' qualifications physically, but he convinced a Marine recruiter that his knowledge of Japanese would be extremely helpful. Gabaldon served in the 2nd Marine Division and deployed to invade Saipan in mid-June of 1944. It was a bloody, twenty-four day battle in mountains and caves, where the 32,000 Japanese troops had plenty of room to hide. The Marines were fierce, however, and Gabaldon, who did like to fight, recalled killing more than thirty enemy Japanese on his first day of combat.

One night, Gabaldon left his post and searched in the extremely dangerous, enemy-held jungle for Japanese troops. He convinced two of them to surrender to him, a brave and remarkable feat, made more astonishing by the fact that the Japanese were known to be very unlikely to surrender under any circumstances. The Japanese typically fought to the death. The next night, Gabaldon brought in fifty prisoners. Gabaldon used various means *to persuade them but mainly promised them humane treatment if they sur-rendered. In all Gabaldon took more than 1,000 prisoners. He was honor-ably discharged in 1945, after being wounded by machine gun fire in Saipan. Gabaldon's commanding officer, Captain John Schwabe, nominated him for the Congressional Gold Medal of Honor, but he received the Silver Cross in-stead. In 1960, a tall, blue-eyed, Irish-American actor named Jeffrey Hunter portrayed Gabaldon in a famous Hollywood movie,* Hell to Eternity, *After the movie's release, people wondered why Gabaldon had not been more highly decorated, and he was then awarded the Navy Cross, the next highest honor after the Medal of Honor. There have been many efforts to fulfill Schwabe's original request and have the Medal of Honor awarded to Gabaldon, but to no avail. Gabaldon, who died in 2006, was known as the Pied Piper of Saipan.*

The Service of Native Americans in the War and The Navajo Code Talkers

When Japan attacked the U.S at Pearl Harbor, Native Americans rallied to protect their homeland. More than 45,000 Native Americans enlisted in the military during the war, and stories of their bravery and devotion grew into tall tales. Some say that natives stood outside in the rain waiting hours to enlist and showed up at enlistment centers with guns so they could get started fighting as soon as possible. Native Americans saw combat in battles throughout the entire war, in Europe, Africa and Asia, and earned three Congressional Gold Medals of Honor and numerous other awards.

In early 1942, Navy Staff Sergeant Philip Johnston learned about a group of Native Americans in the Army in Louisiana who, instead of using code, spoke their own, little known language to send secret war messages. Johnston had grown up in a missionary family on a Navajo reservation in Flagstaff, Arizonia, and could speak a bit of Navajo. He suggested that the Navy employ members of the Navajo Tribe to send messages in battle. He pointed out that very few non-Navajos knew the language and that it did not have a written form – the chances of the enemy learning the Navajo language were virtually zero. The Marine Corps adopted the idea, and Johnston recruited thirty young men from the reservation in Flagstaff. One recruit dropped out, and the group has ever since been known as the "Original 29."

The recruits were sworn into the Marines, sent to boot camp, and worked with cryptographers to take the Navajo language and encode it. For instance, an "observation plane" was the Navajo word for "owl," and "bombs" were "eggs." The Code Talkers memorized the code and got to work.

Eventually, more than four hundred Code Talkers served in the Marines, relaying orders and information over field radios and telephones. From the time they began serving in the summer of 1942 until the end of the war, they worked in every major Marine operation in the Pacific. During the first two days of the Battle for Iwo Jima, six Navajo Code Talkers worked twenty-four hours a day sending and receiving messages. They never made one error. Major Howard Connor, 5th Marine Division Signal Officer stated, "Were it not for the Navajos, the Marines would never have taken Iwo Jima."

The Code Talkers' work was declassified in 1968. In 2000, Congress passed legislation awarding the Original 29 the Congressional Gold Medal of Honor, which was presented to the last four living members of the group by President George W. Bush in 2001.

Navajo Code Talkers being sworn into the Marine Corps.
Photo courtesy of the U.S. National Archives.

General MacArthur coming ashore onto Leyte, in the Philippines, as the Luzon Campaign begins.
Photo courtesy of the U.S. National Archives, number 111-SC-407101.

8

New Guinea, the War in the Pacific and the Service of Technical Sergeant Paul E. Boyer, U.S. Army Air Forces

Lt. General Douglas MacArthur, a legendary veteran of World War I, ran the southwest part of the Allied effort in the Pacific. MacArthur had retired from the U.S. military and was training the Filipino Army when the U.S. was attacked at Pearl Harbor and entered the war. MacArthur was reinstated into the U.S. Army and placed in charge of Army operations in the southwest Pacific.

MacArthur's command in the Philippines had been devastated in Japan's December attack in the Pacific. President Roosevelt ordered MacArthur to retreat to Australia and convinced the Philippine president to move his government temporarily to the U.S. The people of the Philippines were left under siege by terrifying Japanese troops. When MacArthur stated, "I shall return," that utterance became a rallying cry and a beacon of hope for the Philippine people. They endured the horror of the Japanese occupation with faith in MacArthur's words.

After MacArthur made his famous promise, he began to plan Operation Island Hopping. Under this operation, MacArthur's troops successfully pushed the Japanese out of the southwest Pacific, forcing them to retreat home. After a lull in Pacific fighting after the Battle of Midway, Operation Island Hopping began in earnest in April 1944, in New Guinea, the second largest island in the world after Greenland.

With nearly impenetrable jungle thickets, scorching temperatures and even a history of head-hunting rituals, New Guinea is the kind of tropical locale you might find in a horror movie. A jungle-covered mountain range runs across the middle of the island, and where the jungles end, the swamps begin. The U.S. and its allies fought against tough Japanese forces here from 1942 to 1945, and the harsh conditions were an enemy in themselves. The Allies carried sixty-pound packs through swamps with mud as sticky as glue, under storms dropping six to ten inches of rain a day. Many suffered from malaria and other dangerous tropical diseases. Bedtime provided no real rest – troops often slept in mud-filled trenches to avoid Japanese bombs or in barracks with rats running overhead.

The majority of Allied soldiers in New Guinea and the other Pacific islands – Americans, Australians and Pacific Islanders, for the most part -- did not personally fight the Japanese but instead worked in the harsh terrain there to support those who did engage. For each soldier in direct combat, there were seven to eight men on support, all in danger's way – doing the work of building bases and air strips, moving supplies, fighting malaria and, in the case of Technical Sergeant Paul E. Boyer, keeping planes running and in the air. Boyer, who enlisted in the U.S. Army Air Forces (which became the U.S. Air Force at the end of the war) in 1942, at the age of nineteen, survived bomb attacks, Japanese strafes and malaria while serving in New Guinea and elsewhere in the Pacific.

Boyer, who was born and raised in Malone, New York, a small town near Syracuse, enlisted in response to Pearl Harbor. Like many people, he was very patriotic and felt outraged by the attack. He wanted to serve in order to help protect his country.

Although Boyer had wanted to be a pilot when he enlisted, he figured that would not be possible because he wore glasses, and he was right about that. He tested high on mechanical aptitude, which was not surprising because his father was an auto mechanic and had taught him to work with his hands. After basic training, Boyer was sent to mechanics' school outside of Lincoln City, Nebraska.

Lincoln was a friendly city, and the residents there were very supportive of the troops. On Thanksgiving Day of 1942, in Lincoln, some very kind people stopped at the USO and invited Boyer and a couple of his buddies to their home for Thanksgiving dinner. People all across the U.S. invited troops to their homes at holidays and at other times. That meant a lot to the boys.

Boyer did very well at mechanics' school and was selected for specialist training at the Douglas Aircraft Plant in Santa Monica, California, to learn about the A-20 twin-engine bomber. Douglas was an enormous plant, and Boyer was thrilled to be there, watching the hundreds of laborers working round-the-clock shifts, putting together these glorious-looking aircraft. The workers were very friendly and helpful, and they were impressed that Boyer was going to be stationed in a war zone, helping to keep the planes running safely. It was a bit of a heady experience for the young man. He was proud to have such an important job. Boyer observed an A-20 as it was manufactured from start to finish, which took about a month, and then was assigned to the 417th Bomb Group of the Fifth Air Force, which was formed in Oklahoma City, Oklahoma, in March of 1943.

After a few months of flight training in Oklahoma and Louisiana, Boyer, now a crew chief, and his group were sent to Camp Stoneman in California. Here the troops attended to the last-minute details of heading off to war. They underwent vaccinations and dental and medical examinations and had their last wills and testaments formalized.

On January 1, 1944, three weeks after arriving at Camp Stoneman, Boyer and his group were told to prepare to ship out immediately. Phone calls and telegrams were forbidden. People were scared. One man jumped into the river and was caught and hauled away in a strait jacket. A 1st Sergeant shot himself in the foot and was locked up by the security detail.

Boyer and his group set out for the twenty-three day voyage to New Guinea, taking a zigzag route. Japanese ships patrolled the waters, attacking any U.S. ships that they spotted. Boyer was somewhat nervous about getting hit by torpedoes out in the ocean. He was also worried about what he would be facing in New Guinea, wondering if he would survive, but he was a serious young man and knew that the U.S. had to prevent Japan from taking over the Pacific. Some of the guys had a simpler viewpoint and just wanted to shoot some Japanese, the enemy that had attacked the U.S.

Boyer arrived in New Guinea at the end of January of 1944. The Seabees (Navy construction battalions) and Army engineers were cutting through the jungle and building a runway out of interlocking metal pavers. Using scythes, the natives helped cut down the Kunai grass, which can grow to be taller than a person. When the U.S.-built planes arrived from Australia, it was quite a sight – more than seventy planes filled the sky. For the next few months, the airmen flew two missions a day, trying to bomb Japan off the island. The air and ground men often slept outside their base in trenches when the Japanese were bombing their quarters. At one point, Boyer caught malaria and spent time in a field hospital.

In April, Boyer and his fellow troops geared up for one of the first major battles in General MacArthur's Operation Island Hopping – taking a large air-base in Japanese-occupied Hollandia, in Dutch New Guinea. The mission's air time – 4 1/2 to 5 hours – was about the limit the planes could fly before having to return to base for refueling, so there was not much of a margin for error or other problems.

The mission was going well until the weather turned bad. On April 16, several days into the operation, severe thunderstorms broke out while the planes were returning to their bases. Trying to fly around the storms, planes ran short on fuel. Crews had to bail out into the jungle. A B-25 Bomber and a P-38 Fighter landed at opposite ends of the airstrip and crashed into each other.

With the airstrip unavailable, incoming planes were told they could not land. The aircrews yelled into their radios, "We're bailing out, so send the PBYs!" -- the PBY Catalina was an amphibious aircraft used for search and rescue missions and for other roles. "PB" meant "Patrol Bomber" and "Y" was the military designation for Consolidated Aircraft, the manufacturer of the amphibious airship.

After landing in the dense jungle, the crews hoped to be found and res-cued before being captured by the Japanese, a fate likely worse than death. Boyer and most of his buddies were more afraid of being taken prisoner than of dying. They had been told about the brutal treatment of American prison-ers of war in Japanese hands.

Thirty-seven aircraft were destroyed or went missing that day, and April 16, 1944, is still known as "Black Sunday" in the U.S. Air Force. Back at home, however, the entire American nation was dedicating itself to the war effort. The U.S. could easily replace destroyed planes and other equipment, and it did so. The U.S. continued to pound away in the Pacific, pushing the Japanese out of the islands it had attacked and occupied.

A few months after Black Sunday, with heavy losses of troops and equip-ment and without the means to replace them, the Japanese began suicide missions, also known as Kamikaze missions. Kamikaze pilots all supposedly volunteered for these missions so that they could die as martyrs for their country. Elaborate rituals honoring the pilots typically were held as the missions began, and then the Kamikaze pilots would take off in planes full of bombs and dive into Allied ships. The Kamikaze pilots faced certain death. Boyer's convoy was attacked by Kamikazes on its way to his group's new base in Mindanao, Philippines, in late December, and one plane just missed the bow of his ship.

The Japanese portrayed the Kamikaze pilots as heroes, but Boyer had a different perspective. One night in December of 1944, a U.S. plane shot down a small Japanese plane on the beach near Boyer's base. When the infantry went in to take the pilot into custody, they found the Japanese pilot shackled to the plane's rudder by his feet.

Boyer visited the Philippine capital of Manila, after its liberation in March of 1945. The Allies defeated the Japanese there after the fierce, month-long Battle of Manila, allowing MacArthur to keep his famous promise to the people of the Philippines. Boyer enjoyed seeing streets and buildings again – even if most had been destroyed or damaged -- after almost a year in the Pacific jungles.

A chief characteristic of the Island Hopping Operation was to attack strategically important but less heavily defended islands, or "hit them where they aren't'" as MacArthur put it. Nevertheless, almost 4,000 U.S. troops died or were captured and nearly 17,000 suffered injuries in carrying out the operation.

Technical Sergeant Boyer's story concludes in Chapter 24.

The Douglas Plant under Camouflage

During the war, the Douglas Aircraft Plant in Santa Monica, California, employed over 33,000 people working three shifts a day, seven days a week. Amazingly, the entire plant and its grounds were under camouflage to prevent detection from the air by U.S. enemies. The plant's owner, Donald Douglas, had his architect and engineer work with movie set designers from Warner Bros. Studios to make the site look like a residential area. They covered the plant, hangars and parking lots with more than 5 million square feet of chicken wire and burlap and on top of it built a "town" of fake houses and garages made of lightweight wood and marked out mock streets and sidewalks with paint. From the air, the plant looked like a typical Santa Monica neighborhood.

Camp Stoneman

Camp Stoneman, in Pittsburgh, California, was the base from which more than one million troops were deployed to fight the War in the Pacific. The camp was built in 1942 on a strategically located site so that it was accessible by water, rail and highway. Two train lines, the Southern Pacific and the Santa Fe, served the area, and the San Joaquin River, which feeds into the San Francisco Bay, was one mile away.

The 2,500 acre camp ran on a massive scale with 346 barracks housing sixty-three men each, fourteen recreation halls, thirteen mess halls, a chapel, a fire department, a meat-cutting plant and more. Troops were given medical and dental examinations – there were forty-five dental chairs. All clothing, weapons and equipment were inspected, even shoelaces, and there was a twenty-four-hour shoe repair and tailor service. Troops were lectured on chemical warfare, first aid, the rules aboard ship, how to abandon ship, and more. Personnel files were updated and last wills and testaments sworn to.

Helping the troops cope with the stress they faced, the camp included gyms, boxing rings, a baseball field, a pool and a bowling alley. Movie stars such as Groucho Marx, Red Skelton and Lucille Ball entertained there.

The camp was named after Major General George Stoneman, whose storied life included serving as the sixteenth governor of California, having his home burned down by political enemies, and dying a pauper. In 1865, he led Union cavalry troops across six southern states in a highly controversial raid. While the camp named for Stoneman was closed after the Korean War, his name lives on in the lyrics of the rock song, "The Night They Drove Dixie Down," written by Robbie Robertson and released by his group The Band in 1969: "Virgil Cain is the name, and I served on the Danville train. 'Til Stoneman's cavalry came and tore up the tracks again."

Two LSTs (Landing Ship, Tanks) land troops on Leyte. LCIs (Landing Craft, Infantry) landed troops in the same manner.
Photo courtesy of the U.S. National Archives, number 26-G-3738.

9

The Luzon Campaign, the Landing Craft Infantry and the Service of Gunner's Mate Rudolph J. Rolenz, U.S. Navy

In the spring of 1944, just as Boyer was living through Black Sunday in New Guinea, the U.S. Joint Chiefs of Staff were planning the massive invasion of the Japanese homeland, which was scheduled for the autumn of 1945: Operation Downfall. Japan was expecting an invasion and was training even children and the elderly to fight to the death. The U.S. expected casualties on both sides to run into the hundreds of thousands. Should the U.S. base the operation in the Philippines or on the Chinese island of Formosa? MacArthur argued for the Philippines.

Japan has few natural resources, so it was dependent upon shipments of munitions, oil, food and other essentials. The Philippines, which is a chain of islands, or archipelago, lies across shipping lanes that Japan relied upon. MacArthur's plan was to take back the archipelago and cut Japan off from its supplies. He also would be able to keep his famous promise – "I shall return" – to the people of the Philippines who had endured horrors under Japanese occupation. In July he was given the go-ahead to liberate the islands, focusing on an invasion of Luzon, in the central Philippines, to take place in December of 1944.

Fighting in the Pacific was always fierce, as the Japanese fought to the death, rarely surrendering. Taking back the Philippines would be especially brutal because Japan needed to keep the island at all costs.

The Battle of Luzon in the Philippines was one of the largest battles in the Pacific Theater of the war. Gunner's Mate Rudolph J. ("Rudy") Rolenz, worked one of the five 20 mm guns mounted aboard an LCI ship as he and his crewmates stormed onto the beaches of Luzon as a part of the enormous offensive.

Rolenz was working at a tire company in Akron, Ohio, when the U.S. entered the war. He was eligible for a draft deferment because his company manufactured military equipment for the national defense program, but he decided to enlist upon reflection that the thirty people he supervised at work were all women – the men were off fighting the war. He did not want to be left behind while all the other young men served their country. Someone at work had connections with the Navy, so he thought he would enlist in that branch. He didn't want to go into the Army and march.

Rolenz enlisted in the Navy in January of 1943 and had three days to get his affairs in order before the Navy sent him to the Great Lakes Naval Station, located in North Chicago, Illinois, for basic training. More than one million Navy personnel trained at the enormous Great Lakes Naval Station.

Next, the Navy sent Rolenz to the Amphibious Training Base at Little Creek, Virginia, which had just been established at the beginning of the war to train troops in the relatively new tactic of amphibious assault. It was a rustic, swampy place located on an inlet on the south shore of the Atlantic Ocean's Chesapeake Bay. Rolenz and the others in his group were put into operations on how to hit the beach in their ships, drop the ramps on their ships, and send the soldiers in to fight.

Landing Craft Infantry (LCIs) are the small, heavily armed ships that do the extremely dangerous work of carrying Marines and soldiers right onto the beaches where the enemy awaits. On D-Day in Normandy, throughout the Pacific and everywhere the U.S. made amphibious landings, ships like Rolenz's *USS LCI (L) 436*, would pull up near the beach, open large doors, let down ramps into the water, and amphibiously land armed troops, usually onto heavily defended beaches.

The smallest seaworthy ship in the war, an LCI was about 160 feet long and about 23 feet wide, with a crew of about 50. LCI crewmembers got a lot of ribbing from sailors on the big ships, making fun of the LCI's small size, but the LCI crews were brave. They worked right in the middle of battle like the combat troops they carried.

When not getting shot at, mortared or bombed by the enemy, crew members aboard LCIs were often seasick because LCIs were flat on the bottom, a design that allowed them to land on beaches but made them rock at even the slightest ocean wave.

Rolenz was assigned to serve aboard the *LCI (L) 436* under Commander Joseph Witherspoon, who ran a tight ship. Like many successful Navy men, Witherspoon demanded that his ship be kept meticulously clean and that his crew remain disciplined down to the last detail of their clothing and personal grooming. They even had to keep their hats on all the time. Out on the sizzling hot deck of the ship in the Pacific, Rolenz often felt like his hair was going to burn right off his head under his hat. Rolenz swore that if he survived the war, he would never wear a hat again.

In early 1944, under Witherspoon's command, *LCI (L) 436* made more than two-dozen amphibious troop landings in the Bismarck Archipelago Operation and in the Western New Guinea Operation. Next, Rolenz, Witherspoon and the rest of the men on the ship prepared to help General MacArthur keep his famous promise to the people of the Philippines.

The Battle of Luzon was preceded by the U.S. amphibious landing on Leyte, which gave the U.S. a foothold on land. The battle began in October of 1944, with a two-day bombardment of Japanese defenses on Leyte by U.S. forces, careful of MacArthur's orders to avoid harm to civilians and civilian property. Next, in one of the largest assemblages of naval assault craft and warships ever gathered in the Pacific, MacArthur and his troops landed on Leyte and began the fight against the Japanese. MacArthur walked ashore in knee-deep water and, once he was on the island, he took a portable radio and announced to the Filipinos that he was keeping his promise to return.

> *This is the Voice of Freedom, General MacArthur speaking. People of the Philippines: I have returned. By the grace of Almighty God our forces stand again on Philippine soil – soil consecrated in the blood of our two peoples. We have come, dedicated and committed to the task of destroying every vestige of enemy control over your daily lives....*
>
> *Rally to me.... As the lines of battle roll forward to bring you within the zone of operations, rise and strike! For future generations of your sons and daughters, strike! In the name of your sacred dead, strike! Let no heart be faint. Let every arm be steeled....*

63

Then, the U.S. planned to land on Mindoro, which was needed as a base of operations for taking Luzon. The biggest threat to the amphibious landing at Mindoro was Japanese Kamikaze pilots. By the end of the battle for Leyte, the Japanese had started suicide missions. On December 13, two days before the landings on Mindoro were to take place, a Kamikaze hit the *USS Nashville*, in the Philippines, killing more than 130 men and wounding more than 190. Kamikazes also damaged several LCIs, though not the one Rolenz served aboard.

Rolenz was nervous about the Kamikazes, but he knew that the LCIs had heavy support when they hit the beaches. They were backed up by aircraft carriers and destroyers, but it was still very dangerous -- one of the LCIs near Rolenz was bombed during a landing. Rolenz' LCI successfully landed its troops in mid December, and the long Battle of Luzon began.

Japan's strategy in the Luzon campaign was a passive war of attrition. Japanese troops scattered throughout the jungle hitting at U.S. troops basically like snipers. It was tough fighting. By the end of March, the U.S. had driven out the Japanese from all key locations and declared the Philippines liberated, though many Japanese soldiers were hiding there. The Filipino people celebrated and cheered the soldiers in the streets.

Rolenz and his buddies knew they still had a lot of fighting to get through, but they felt like there was an end in sight.

Gunner's Mate Rolenz' story concludes in Chapter 24.

WAVES recruiting poster.
Photo courtesy of the U.S. Navy.

10

The WAVES and the Service of First Class Aviation Machinist Mate Fran Lokey Phelps, U.S. Navy

Frances Lokey Phelps was born on a plantation in Alabama's Black Belt region, an area known for its rich, black soil. When the stock market crashed and the Great Depression began, Phelps' family lost everything -- their savings had all been tied up in cotton futures. Phelps' father got work running a farm for a relative in Shelby County, Alabama. The farm didn't make money, but it provided food for the family. There was a river near the property, and Phelps' father ran a ferry on it. That brought some money in so they could afford to buy a few things, like clothing, and didn't have to wear clothes made out of flour sacks like most of the kids in the area. Phelps' experiences on the farm prepared her for success in serving in the U.S. Navy.

Phelps grew up shadowing her father on the farm, just as her older brother and sister had done before her, and she learned how to fix anything that needed repair. During the Depression, most people repaired everything that broke – they didn't have money to buy new things. When she wasn't helping her father, Phelps ran around on the farm playing sports with the other kids – underprivileged boys who Phelps' parents took into their home and the children of the tenant farmers on the property, who were African American. The notion of black and white children playing together in the segregated Deep South in the 1930's may surprise people, but Phelps is full of surprises.

The farm not only nurtured her athleticism and mechanical aptitude, it was also the place where she became interested in airplanes. "I had a friend in high school who had a plane. He would fly over to my house and land in my backyard and we would go out flying. That was a lot of fun. I probably listed that as an interest on my Navy application," Phelps recalls.

When the U.S. entered the war, only twenty years had passed since women had earned the right to vote. Many people still believed that women were inferior to men in any number of ways and that military service should be restricted to men only. Some women took exception to that notion, including Phelps. Phelps enlisted in the Navy for the same reason that many men enlisted – she was a patriot who wanted to help the war effort. Always mechanically inclined – years after the war, she helped build a dune buggy that her son drove in college – Phelps tested off the charts on the Navy's mechanical aptitude test and was assigned to work as a Naval aircraft mechanic. She loved every minute of her service.

The very first women affiliated with the U.S. Navy were the Catholic Sisters of the Holy Cross, who worked as nurses in the American Civil War. Women officially joined the Navy in 1908, when the Navy Nurse Corps was established, and World War I marked the first time that women served in the Navy in roles other than nursing. During that war, more than 10,000 Navy Yeomen (F) and 300 Marinettes of the Marine Corps of the Navy served. They performed clerical work for the most part, but some had more sophisticated duties.

World War II brought about an enormous demand for labor, and women were brought back into the Navy in a more expansive role than ever before. In the summer of 1942, Congress passed a bill establishing a Women's Reserve branch of the Naval Volunteer Reserve, which President Roosevelt signed into law. The unit was called the Women Accepted for Volunteer Emergency Service, and it and the women who served in it became known as "WAVES."

For most of the war, WAVES could serve only in the continental U.S. and not on board ships or in combat aircraft, but they held many important jobs. Also, for the first time, women could hold rank in the Navy, and the first female commissioned officer in the Navy, Mildred McAfee, was sworn in as a Naval Reserve Lieutenant Commander and Director of the WAVES. Navy nurses, who did serve in combat zones, were given "relative rank," so they were noncommissioned officers, with rank corresponding with officers' rank. More than 11,000 nurses served in the Navy during World War II.

McAfee got the WAVES program up and running quickly, establishing training programs and accommodations, getting uniforms designed and manufactured, and dealing with all the details of integrating women into a men's organization. Even saluting was an issue because saluting rules are based in part upon how one wears a hat, and customs for hat wearing are different for men and women. A 1943 WAVES newsletter breezily noted when that problem had been resolved. "Because the Feminine Navy wears hats many-a-time where and when men don't, saluting has had complications. But as time and the WAVES march on, those complications have been fairly well ironed out and definite saluting practices established."

Under McAfee's leadership and outstanding organizational talents, twenty-seven thousand women served in the first year of the WAVES. In July of 1943, President Roosevelt marked the first anniversary of the organization with a letter that read, in part:

One year ago today the United States Navy opened to this nation's patriotic womanhood an opportunity for service within its ranks. The wholly voluntary response came in such swelling volume as to constitute a ringing confirmation of the tenet that, in total war, democracy must be fought for and defended by all the people. Once again, the women of this free land stepped forward to prove themselves worthy descendants of those proud pioneer daughters who first nurtured freedom's flame.

Several months after President Roosevelt wrote this letter, Phelps enlisted in the Navy, in December of 1943, as soon as she was old enough to join up. She chose the Navy for two reasons. One, she comes from a long line of Navy people and even has an ancestor who was a sea captain and fought the British in the Revolutionary War. Also, she agreed with the WAVES' mission, that women were there to relieve a man to fight. For each woman who served, one more man could go off to war.

Phelps was sent to boot camp at Hunter College, located in the Bronx Borough of New York City, where most WAVES trained. Basic training was very similar to the men's — marches, tough calisthenics, patrols and inspections, with strict discipline expected at every point. The WAVES learned how the Navy is organized, the ranks and ratings and how and when to salute. Phelps' days as a civilian were over for now. When she and the others arrived at boot camp, their civilian clothes were sent home, and they never wore civilian clothes again until they were discharged from the service.

From Hunter College, Phelps was put on a troop train, in resurrected old cars, and sent to Norman, Oklahoma, to learn aircraft mechanics. They took a circuitous route up through Canada because of fears of espionage. The Navy had chosen Norman as the location of a large Navy facility – it's right in the middle of the U.S. so it could serve both coasts -- and in 1942 transformed the college town, home of the University of Oklahoma, into a small city. The Navy built an airbase, a hospital, an air gunnery school and training school for aviation mechanics, where Phelps trained.

At Norman, Phelps learned how the planes operated, how to spot problems and how to repair any item on the planes. Phelps' class was ninety percent men. Physically, she was small, and the men were always willing to help her with any lifting, so being a woman was never a problem, she felt. She enjoyed school and loved learning aircraft mechanics. She also enjoyed the novelty of military life -- the strict discipline, the inspections of their living quarters, performing night patrols.

After graduating from training with a 3rd class rate (or specialty) as an aircraft mechanic, Phelps was sent to motion picture school and taught how to operate and repair 8, 16 and 35 mm. film projectors so that she could work as a movie projectionist at her new base, the Naval Technical Training Center outside of Memphis, Tennessee. She was paid extra for her work as a projectionist and enjoyed it.

She screened training films and, in the evenings, showed movies for entertainment. She'd get a jeep, drive into Memphis and pick up the cans of film – a movie, a newsreel, a cartoon and a preview, and then drive back to the base and screen the film for the men. It was tricky work, and if she made a mistake, she had to contend with three hundred sailors yelling that they wanted their movie back on. Phelps eventually attained a first class rating, which gave her a supervisory role in aircraft mechanics at the Training Center, and she continued with her projectionist work.

Being a part of the entertainment department allowed Phelps to meet the famous performers who came to put on shows for the sailors. Since it was a large training center, many big stars came to perform. Phelps' favorite was Bob Hope. After they would finish filming his show, he would tell the guys, "Okay, now we can relax and let our hair down." The show would get a little more risqué, by the standards of the day.

The WAVES and the enlisted men spent their free time socializing. They had picnics and bowled and golfed. On weekends, they took busses to the

Peabody Hotel in Memphis and drank beer in a big rec room. Sometimes people drank a bit too much, but otherwise it was just good, clean fun, as Phelps experienced it.

Like Phelps, many WAVES did important work during the war. More than 80,000 WAVES worked in fields such as law, science, technology, intelligence and more. Just twenty years after earning the right to vote, to be equal citizens to men, these women were proving that females were capable of intelligent, skilled work.

Some WAVES worked as airplane control tower operators. They needed to have perfect vision, short reaction times, the ability to work under stress and strong mathematical abilities. Many people believed that women performed better at this job than men. Some WAVES trained at Parachute School in New Jersey and learned to be parachute riggers – inspecting, repairing and packing parachutes. They tested the parachutes by skydiving.

Other WAVES went from boot camp at Hunter College to Washington, D.C. where they worked in cryptology. Cryptographers work on breaking enemy codes and developing codes for their own military to use. WAVES who worked in cryptography dealt with highly classified, top secret information, and only women with the highest integrity were chosen for this service. They were told that speaking about their work outside of approved channels would be an act of treason with a possible penalty of death.

The Navy held secret code training classes in several colleges for women who scored high on aptitude tests and who passed very strict loyalty tests. Coding is mathematical work, and many cryptologists in the Navy had been math teachers and math professors before the war. By February of 1944, nearly 3,000 WAVES worked in intelligence at the Naval Annex in Washington, D.C. Many of them worked on enormous electro-mechanical machines called "Bombes" to decode enemy messages sent using a type of coding machine called "Enigma," the coder favored by the Germans,

When a message was typed into an Engima, which looked like an old-fashioned typewriter in a wooden box, rotors made substitutions for the letters typed in and thus encoded the information. In 1940, a British mathematician named Alan Turing, one of the fathers of computer science, invented the Bombe, an electro-mechanical machine – not a computer -- that could help decipher Enigma codes. A couple of years later, Britain gave the U.S. permission to use the Bombe, and WAVES and civilian cryptologists travelled to Dayton, Ohio, to help build 120 Bombes, which were then sent to the Naval Annex in Washington. There the WAVES worked around the clock operating the machines in hot, loud rooms. The working conditions were very challenging.

Stress was high because mistakes could cost lives, and sleep was a problem for women working the evening and overnight shifts because they had to sleep in the barracks during the day. With the "can do" attitude that characterized much of the war effort, The WAVES met the challenges of their jobs. The Bombe significantly contributed to the Allied victory in World War II, in large part by decoding German naval communications. The WAVES who worked in cryptology saved countless American lives.

First Class Aviation Machinist Mate Phelps' story concludes in Chapter 24.

A WAVE working on a Bombe machine.
Photo courtesy of the National Security Administration.

U.S. Army Air Forces' raid on a Focke-Wulf plant in 1943.
Photo courtesy of the U.S. National Archives, number 208-YE-7.

11

Big Week and the Service of Lawrence J. Dunn, Sr., Staff Sergeant, U.S. Army Air Forces

By early 1944, the massive plans for D-Day were well under way, and the 8th and 15th U.S. Army Air Forces in Europe had just been reorganized and reestablished as the U.S. Strategic Air Forces. The USSTAF intended to weaken Germany's ability to defend the beaches of Normandy on D-Day and, eventually, to destroy Germany's air power completely. The strategic bombing campaign began in earnest on February 20, 1944, in a six-day bomb attack on Germany's airplane industry that came to be known as "Big Week." Big Week was hugely successful – the U.S. dropped 10,000 tons of bombs on aircraft factories and other key sites and destroyed more than six hundred German fighter planes. With its ability to manufacture aircraft seriously crippled and unable to replace the fighter pilots it lost, the German Air Force, the *Luftwaffe,* never fully recovered from Big Week.

Staff Sergeant Lawrence J. Dunn, fresh out of high school, joined up with the 15th Air Force just as it was moving from Africa to Italy. Growing up, Dunn was a quiet but popular boy who was nicknamed "Bud" and who loved to play basketball. His parents raised him along with his two sisters and brother in Naugatuck, Connecticut. During Dunn's senior year, his high school basketball team won the State and New England basketball championships, and Dunn and his teammates received fine wristwatches as their awards.

After Dunn graduated from high school in June of 1942, he was drafted into the Army, and six months later, he was off to basic training. He was accepted into the Army Air Forces and trained as a gunner on the Boeing B-17, which was known as "The Flying Fortress" because of its heavy armor and huge firepower. After a short leave home to visit his parents in September of 1943, Dunne departed for Africa, to war, just before his twentieth birthday.

Dunn was assigned to work as one of two waist gunners on his plane. His job was to stand at a window located near the tail, back-to-back with the other waist gunner and shoot at enemy planes. The waist gunners operated twin 50 mm caliber machine guns that were mounted at their open windows. Later, B-17s were fitted with Plexiglas windows, but Dunn's plane was an earlier B-17. Standing in open windows, the waist gunners were in the most dangerous position on the plane. Dunn's parents were worried about their son but had no idea of how much danger he faced.

The 15th Air Force was based first in Tunisia, in Africa, and then after Italy surrendered to the Allies in September of 1943, the 15th moved across the Mediterranean to a base in Foggia, Italy, in December. Based out of Africa and then Italy, Dunn completed twenty-four missions as a waist gunner in a B-17 heavy bomber named *Indianapolis War Bird*.

Five days into the Big Week campaign, on February 24, 1944, a cloudy, wintry day in Italy, Dunn prepared for his twenty-fifth mission, and it was to be a long one. They were to cross the Alps and bomb the Aircraft Components Parts Factory located in Steyr, in the Danube River Valley. The factory was controlled by the Germans. Due to the length of the mission – Steyr is located almost 800 miles from Foggia – Dunn's B-17 carried extra fuel that day, as did many of the other bombers and fighters.

A "Tokyo tank" is what the men called the tank for the extra fuel. It was located in the bomb bay, so they could carry about half the normal bomb load if they had the extra fuel. If someone said he was carrying a Tokyo tank, that meant he was headed for a long mission. One of the biggest dangers on a long mission is running out of fuel. On one of Dunn's previous missions they ran so low on fuel that the pilot ordered them to jettison everything from the plane – even their guns – and they ran out of their last drops of fuel on the runway as they landed.

Four B-17 bomb groups would head out to Steyr that day, and they needed escort. The B-17 was called "The Flying Fortress," but it had to be protected in the air, as sad experience had proven. Casualties on long-range B-17 missions without escort had been far too high, culminating on October 14, 1943, about the time Dunn arrived in Africa. On that day, known as "Black Friday," sixty B-17s were shot down in a raid over Schweinfurt, Germany, and more than 600 U.S. airmen were lost.

Ordinarily, about two hundred fighter planes would protect Dunn's group on a mission. The mission to Steyr, however, would be different because of the fuel issues. Even though the fighters carried extra fuel, it was not enough to allow them to stay with the B-17s for the entire mission. The airmen knew this. Another problem would arise, however, that they didn't know about ahead of time. The B-17s were supposed to be followed by a group of B-24 bombers, but the B-24s would never arrive, due to the bad weather.

Dunn's 2nd Bomb Group was the last of the four bomb groups on the mission to Steyr, and his squadron of seven planes was the last of the bomb group, so Dunn's squadron was the last of the last, the most exposed planes on the mission. Without the B-24s, Dunn's squadron would be sitting ducks once the fighters had to pull away.

As with the start of all of his missions, Dunn was aware of his level of nervousness. In his opinion, it was good to be a little bit scared but not too frightened. Dunn and his nine crewmates flew at an altitude of 10,000 feet into Austria, to save fuel, and ascended to 25,000 feet, for safety, as they neared their target. The B-17 was not pressurized, so the men wore oxygen masks. They also wore heated, electric suits because the plane was frigid -- temperatures of 50 degrees below zero, *Fahrenheit*, at 25,000 feet were recorded, and Dunn and Webb, the other waist gunner, were particularly cold because they stood in open windows. The heated suits were plugged into electric outlets on the plane, and many men on these missions reported that their suits did not work. Dunn's fingers were usually numb with cold on his missions.

From Dunn's perspective, the mission felt like a massacre. As soon as the U.S. fighters turned back, the German planes appeared. He could tell that the Germans were taking down each U.S. plane one by one. Several German fighters would attack one bomber until the plane was disabled, and then move on to the next one. The Germans were attacking in groups of four to six *Focke-Wulf* 190 fighters, armed with machine guns, and they were also firing long-range rockets and launching aerial bombs. Dunn knew he would be a victim. He knew his plane would be hit, but he was determined to fight with all he had. He and his crewmates wanted to take a whole lot of Germans down with them.

Dunn fired like mad as his plane was hit over and over with gunfire and shelling. The other waist gunner on his plane, Webb, was shot in the stomach with a 20 mm shell and died immediately. After he was hit, Webb fell to the floor of the tiny space he shared with Dunn, and as he fell, his body knocked into Dunn, pulling Dunn's headset off. This caused Dunn to lose contact with the rest of the crew. Dunn continued fighting, standing next to his friend's dead body.

Soon the plane was on fire, though Dunn, alone in his compartment in the back without his headset on, did not know this. When the plane became engulfed in flames, the pilot ordered, "Bail Out." Dunn was unable to hear the order, so he continued firing. He didn't realize that he was alone in the plane.

Firing his guns from inside the unmanned, burning plane, which was flying on autopilot, Dunn suddenly noticed the door to the radio room swinging open. He saw the empty pilot's chamber – he was alone on the plane! Dunn secured his parachute, ran up to the front of the plane, past two more dead buddies, and bailed out through the bomb bay, open because the pilot had jettisoned the bombs when he had bailed out. Dunn was floating down through the sky when a German fighter plane came by and shot hundreds of holes in his parachute. Dunn plunged to the ground. He landed on snow-covered rock and ruptured his knee.

Dunn had landed in an open field, and before he had time to figure out where to hide, five Austrian policemen showed up to arrest him. The policemen, oddly, were very nervous, but this did not surprise Dunn. He had been briefed on this. A widespread rumor in Europe had it that all U.S. airmen were Chicago gangsters, a terrifying group of criminals that had gained worldwide notoriety in the 1930's.

Dunn spent the night in the local jail, and the next day he was sent to Frankfurt, Germany, to the prisoner of war – POW – processing center, where he was photographed and processed according to international law. Dunn was now a part of the *Luftwaffe* prison system. The *Luftwaffe* operated six POW camps for airmen who had been captured, segregating the officers from the enlisted men. Being an airman was widely considered a prestigious position by the Germans and the Allies, and some enemy airmen reported that they felt a certain kinship with each other as fellow airmen.

Dunn was interrogated at the *Luftwaffe* Aircrew Association, where all captured airmen were questioned. The Germans figured they were more likely to get the airmen to reveal secrets while they were still in shock from having been shot down and taken into custody. Allied medical personnel provided medical treatment to the captured crewmembers. Dunn received medical attention on February 28, 1944, four days after rupturing his knee.

Dunn learned from some other prisoners that the mission had been a success for the USSTAF, but that Dunn's entire squadron had gone down.

On March 15, 1944, Dunn's parents received a Western Union telegram informing them that their son "HAS BEEN REPORTED MISSING IN ACTION OVER AUSTRIA IF FURTHER DETAILS OR FURTHER INFORMATION ARE RECEIVED YOU WILL BE PROMPTLY NOTIFIED."

A set of international treaties known as the Geneva Conventions is aimed in part at protecting prisoners of war. Germany had a reputation for complying with the Geneva Conventions during the war, and the *Luftwaffe's* prisons were considered by some to be superior to the other German prison camps, but German mistreatment of its prisoners was widespread, especially toward the end of the war.

After the war, the U.S. War Department compiled evidence of Germany's egregious violations of the Geneva Conventions, and charges of war crimes were brought against Germans for their treatment of the Allied prisoners. The U.S. soldiers who liberated the prison camps, however, had more than sufficient evidence of war crimes – many of them were heartbroken as they freed their sick, emaciated brothers from the prisons, particularly when they recalled the decent treatment they had shown to their German prisoners. Dunn and the other prisoners with whom he was detained endured brutal conditions.

Dunn spent the rest of the war trying to stay alive in German prison camps. He survived the camps and the infamous Forced Marches, but just barely.

Sergeant Dunn's story concludes in Chapter 24.

Supreme Commander of the Allied Forces General Dwight D. Eisenhower, who would later become the 34th President of the United States, briefs paratroopers on D-Day.
Photo courtesy of the U.S. National Archives, number 531217.

12

D-Day and Sergeant Krom's Story Continues

Hitler had an evil genius for politics and for creating a devoted following of people, but he was not an adept military leader. After a series of bad decisions and miscalculations on Hitler's part, the spring of 1944 and the approach of D-Day found the Germans embroiled in war in Russia and spread too thinly there along a massive front. The German army as a whole had lost many troops and run out of replacements; the German air force was almost completely destroyed; the German homeland had taken heavy bombardment; and many of Hitler's top military officials had come to doubt his judgment and abilities. Nevertheless, Hitler controlled most of Europe; his brutal machine of inhumanity surged on; his political acumen could not be underestimated; and he had to be stopped. The operation to eradicate Hitler's power would begin on the beaches of Normandy, France, on D-Day, June 6, 1944.

D-Day was remarkable in every respect: the terrible bloodshed and loss of human life; the sheer enormity of the operation in terms of troops and equipment; the extensive planning, which lasted two years; the deception plan to fool the Germans regarding where and when the invasion would take place; and the critical importance of success when the troops landed on the beaches.

The Allied leaders – U.S. and Britain – had recognized the need for a massive Allied invasion of Europe since late in 1941. By 1942, pockets of liberation efforts in German-controlled countries were taking hold. The Russians were fighting the Germans in the east. Obviously, if the Allies could launch a huge invasion of Western Europe, Germany would have to fight on two large fronts. Roosevelt and Churchill agreed, however, that the operation would have to be colossal in order to succeed and therefore could not to be done until sufficient troops could be trained and the necessary equipment manufactured. In late 1943, Roosevelt and Churchill met in Cairo, Egypt, named General Dwight D. Eisenhower as the Commander of Operation Overlord, and informed Soviet Premiere Joseph Stalin that the invasion would take place in the spring of 1944.

The U.S. became a country of factories churning out war equipment. By D-Day, over one half million planes, tanks, guns and other items – 5 million tons of equipment in all – had been shipped off to England, which had become the largest military base in the world. Troops began arriving in England for training in 1942. By June of 1944, two million troops had assembled there. One and a half million of these troops were from the U.S. British troops numbered about one half million, and Canada and fourteen other countries sent troops as well.

This massive build-up of troops and equipment could not be completely hidden from the Germans, who realized that an attack on Western Europe would be the next logical move by the Allies. Germany had defenses lined up all along the coast of France but would not be able to successfully ward off a massive assault without knowing exactly where the Allies would land. The Allies devised an elaborate deception scheme involving spies, coded messages, fake military bases built by movie crews, and fake troops and equipment, and they pulled off a massive hoax -- Hitler was convinced that the Allies planned their invasion for mid-July and that they would come ashore at Port Calais, France, about 150 miles east of Normandy.

German Field Marshall Erwin Rommel was known as "the Desert Fox" for his remarkable feats in the North Africa campaigns against the Allies. In 1943, Hitler put him in charge of defending the northern coast of France against the expected invasion. Rommel fortified German defenses across the coast and booby-trapped the beaches with every kind of explosive and obstacle he could find -- mortars, shells, mines, barbed wires – and even designed some himself. Rommel believed that the invasion would be won or lost on the beaches – the Allies had to be stopped on the beach, right when they landed, within the first twenty-four hours of the invasion.

Krom was sent to a staging area in southern England at the end of May to get ready for D-Day. He and the others listened to speeches from the commanders at their staging area and received a letter that Eisenhower wrote to the troops:

Soldiers, Sailors and Airmen of the Allied Expeditionary Force!

You are about to embark upon the Great Crusade, toward which we have striven these many months. The eyes of the world are upon you. The hopes and prayers of liberty-loving people everywhere march with you. In company with our brave Allies and brothers-in-arms on other Fronts, you will bring about the destruction of the German war machine, the elimination of Nazi tyranny over the oppressed peoples of Europe, and security for ourselves in a free world.

Your task will not be an easy one. Your enemy is well trained, well equipped and battle-hardened. He will fight savagely.

But this is the year 1944! Much has happened since the Nazi triumphs of 1940-41. The United Nations have inflicted upon the Germans great defeats, in open battle, man-to-man. Our air offensive has seriously reduced their strength in the air and their capacity to wage war on the ground. Our Home Fronts have given us an overwhelming superiority in weapons and munitions of war, and placed at our disposal great reserves of trained fighting men. The tide has turned! The free men of the world are marching together to Victory!

I have full confidence in your courage, devotion to duty and skill in battle. We will accept nothing less than full Victory!

Good Luck! And let us all beseech the blessing of Almighty God upon this great and noble undertaking.

The troops spent the weekend in England aboard the ships that would take them to Normandy. The weather was stormy, so the sea was rough and many men were seasick on the ships as they waited for the operation to begin. Others wrote letters home and cleaned their weapons. Two task forces were charged with bringing the troops from ports all over England, landing them at Normandy, keeping them supplied, and giving them fire support and medical help. Krom crossed the English Channel on the *USS Samuel Chase*, a Coast Guard attack transport ship.

D-Day began in the air, hours before dawn when, under a three-part bombardment plan, Allied bombers struck strategic sites. Just before daybreak, planes dropped more than 20,000 paratroopers and gliders to capture important bridges and establish ground. These men met with gunfire, booby traps and explosives. They suffered such heavy casualties that their gliders came to be called "flying coffins."

Omaha Beach, where Krom would land, was the most heavily defended of the beaches that the Allies would assault on D-Day. There the Germans had constructed eight large concrete bunkers, thirty-five concrete pill boxes, six mortar pits, thirty-five rocket launchers and eighty-five machine gun nests to thwart an Allied landing. Firepower covered the entire beach, and booby traps had been set under the water and on the land. The Germans had a natural advantage as well – their fortifications were set atop bluffs, so they could look down upon the Allied troops coming ashore.

Early in the morning on D-Day, a critical element of the Allied plan to overcome German defenses on Omaha Beach failed: the pre-dawn Air Force bombers that were supposed to take out the German defense along the beach had problems under the cloud cover and missed their targets by three miles. The German fortifications were manned.

As dawn broke, Allied ships began shelling the beaches, and then at about 6:30 a.m., landing craft ships drew close to shore. Smoke from the shelling filled the air, and the morning was cloudy. The men who would be landing each carried about seventy-five pounds of equipment. They had just spent several days aboard ship waiting for this day and had just crossed the English Channel, which was particularly rough and choppy that night. They came close to shore amidst the sound of gunfire and into Rommel's smoke-filled killing grounds. They watched as landing craft ships became impaled on Rommel's obstacles, were blown up by firepower or explosives, or caught fire.

The crafts that did make it intact drew close to shore into waist-high water. As the ramps of the crafts went down, the doors opened and the brave soldiers marched into the water. The Germans opened fire right at them as they exited and simply mowed them down. Men died on the spot or fell, severely wounded, into the water and drowned with their heavy packs on. The doors of the landing crafts through which the troops walked came to be known as "the jaws of death."

By 8:00 a.m., as the tide came in, all of Rommel's booby traps were hidden under the water and deadlier than ever. It was a scene from hell. Dead and injured men, as well as destroyed equipment and debris, filled the water and covered the beach. Men took cover where they could amidst the wrecked equipment. The landings continued.

The first wave of men to walk onto the beaches took the brunt of the German fire. Entire teams of soldiers from these assault groups were killed within minutes. Next came the demolition teams, who managed to blow up channels to make passage lanes through the water but didn't get a chance to mark them before the tide started to come in. They took heavy losses as well: two of the fourteen demolition teams were wiped out almost immediately.

Krom landed at about 9:00 a.m. The noise was deafening, and it was almost impossible to see. At first, the deadly scene was chaotic: most of the officers in the first waves of landings had been killed, and many survivors were stunned into inaction. Troops also got stuck in what were essentially traffic jams caused by human bodies and destroyed equipment. Getting off the beach was imperative, but to get to the relative safety of the seawall, the men had to traverse about 400 yards of open, mined land under heavy German gunfire.

As soldier after soldier took the beach, the Germans kept shelling. Krom didn't think he had much of a chance of surviving. He relied heavily on his training, which had been excellent.

As Krom was coming to shore, his landing craft was hit. Shrapnel struck the driver of his ammunition truck. Eight men were wounded, and water poured in. Krom drove ashore in his truck, which was waterproof, though he had to hold the air intake valve for the carburetor above the water as they drove in. It was awful because he didn't know what he was running over. There were so many bodies. He drove a stranded colonel onto the beach because the colonel's command car had gone underwater. The colonel ordered Krom to pull his car out, and Krom's commanding sergeant told him, "No. Our orders are to get off the beach. I don't care if a *general* wants his car towed." A minute later a shell exploded on the colonel's car. That would have killed them.

It is a wonder, but with bravery, determination and thorough training, American troops prevailed on Omaha Beach. By noon they had a portable dock installed and were bringing trucks in over the water. Krom drove to a staging area in the hedge grows – centuries' old, immense walls of terrain and shrubbery that fenced off fields of farmland. But there was no rest – they took heavy shooting from the Germans at the staging area as well. General Omar Bradley, commander of the U.S. ground forces on D-Day, said that every man who set foot on Omaha Beach that day was a hero.

The massive Normandy invasion continued throughout the day. "My gosh, the sky was dark. There were thousands of planes. You could see guys parachuting out, and they were shooting them down," Krom noticed. The Allies commanded a staggering force of over 13,000 aircraft on D-Day. Upwards of four thousand ships plus several thousand smaller craft streamed across the English Channel, reportedly causing one German soldier to exclaim that there couldn't be that many ships in the world. According to a popular account of the day, an Allied bomber pilot said that as he looked down from his plane, he believed that a person could have walked across the English Channel that day, stepping from ship to ship.

By day's end, more that one hundred thousand men had landed on the 50-mile-long stretch of beaches. The U.S. landed at Utah and Omaha Beaches, and British and Canadian forces landed at Juno, Gold and Sword Beaches. The inclement weather that had made so many Allied troops seasick as they crossed the English Channel had provided a stroke of luck for the Allies. A few weeks earlier, the German Navy had reported that stormy weather would prevent an Allied attack in early June. The Germans relaxed a bit, and on June 5, Rommel went home to Germany to celebrate his wife's birthday and meet with Hitler. He was not there on D-Day to command troops and bring in reinforcements during those critical first twenty-four hours.

The Allies had established a beachhead in German-controlled Europe, making Operation Overlord a success. Thousands gave their lives for the operation. Thousands more were wounded.

Sergeant Krom's story concludes in Chapter 24.

U.S. soldiers disembarking into devastating German fire on the coast of Normandy, France, on D-Day, June 6, 1944. CPhoM. Robert F. Sargent. Photo courtesy of the U.S. National Archives, number 26-G-2343.

Two battleships followed by three cruisers in the Pacific Ocean in January of 1945. Photo courtesy of the U.S. National Archives, number 80-G-59525.

13

Ships in the War
And the Service of Petty Officer Robert Poole, U.S. Navy

From battleships, carriers and cruisers to destroyers, frigates, submarines and more, the sheer size of the U.S. Navy fleet was astounding: the end of World War II saw more than six thousand ships on active duty. Referred to as a "she," a ship typically had a life marked by pomp and ceremony, and like people, ships earned awards in the war. The end of a ship's life is referred to as her "fate." Navy veterans remember their ships very well, and Third Class Petty Officer Bob Poole is no exception. Poole served aboard two ships: the *USS Tuscaloosa*, a heavy cruiser considered to be a fortunate ship as she was never severely damaged in the war, and the *USS Alaska*, a large cruiser that he helped take on her "shakedown cruise" – a test of a new ship's equipment. Poole recalls being aboard the Tuscaloosa as she followed one of the most famous Allied ships of the war: the *RMS Queen Mary*, a once-beautiful, English luxury liner that had been refitted for the war and was used to transport Allied troops and war prisoners.

Instead of waiting to be drafted, Poole enlisted in 1943 at the age of seventeen so that he could choose his service branch. The Navy appealed to him because his uncles were Navy men. He was assigned to the *Tuscaloosa*, which had spent most of her life on neutrality patrol – watching out for hostile operations in the Atlantic after Germany invaded Poland in 1939. The *Tuscaloosa* had been "laid down" in September 1931 in a ceremony held in the shipyard in which she would be built, the New York Shipbuilding Company in Camden, New Jersey.

A ship's construction typically began with the keel, basically a steel back-bone running from the fore to the aft (front to back) of the ship. The "laying of the keel" is the ceremony that marks the beginning of a ship's construction. The *Tuscaloosa's* ceremony, if typical, would have been quite formal, led by a government official, such as a Congressman, who would have carved or written his initials on the keel. Shipbuilders would then have placed the keel into its construction position and an official would have announced that the keel had been "truly and fairly laid."

After the ship's construction, in a formal ceremony marked by a chaplain's prayer and remarks by Navy officers, the *Tuscaloosa* was christened and launched on November 15, 1933. As was typical, her sponsor – who would have announced "I christen thee the *Tuscaloosa*" – was a woman with a connection to the ship's namesake, in this case a niece of the congressman who represented the small city of Tuscaloosa, Alabama, before the U.S. House of Representatives. The christening very likely ended with the sponsor smashing a bottle of champagne against the bow of the ship, and as the ship was launched into the water, most likely a Navy band would have played the song "Anchors Away." Later, in another ceremony, the *Tuscaloosa* earned the title USS (United States Ship) on August 17, 1934, when the Navy commissioned her.

Poole enlisted in Chicago, Illinois, and trained there at the Great Lakes Naval Training Station. Located a thousand miles from the nearest ocean, this station trained over a third of the Navy's personnel in the war, more than a million people. The Navy sent Poole to Boston, Massachusetts, and he went aboard the *Tuscaloosa* at the Boston Navy Yard. It was the summer of 1943, and the British Prime Minister, Winston Churchill, was visiting the United States, discussing tactics with President Roosevelt and addressing a joint session of the U.S. Congress on the war. Afterwards, the Prime Minister traveled to Nova Scotia, Canada, and Poole remembers that the *Tuscaloosa* followed the *Queen Mary* there. Poole and his crewmates hoped for a glimpse of Churchill, rumored to have been on the ship as she was reportedly the only ship on which he would travel.

Churchill's faith in the ship was well placed. The *RMS Queen Mary* and her sister ship the *RMS Queen Elizabeth*, also a converted luxury liner painted grey, were the pride of the Royal fleet. ("RMS" stands for "royal mail service" and denotes ships certified to carry the royal mail.) They arguably were the largest troop carriers in the war, with a capacity for more than 15,000 passengers, and the fastest, with an average speed of 26 knots. Nicknamed the Gray Ghosts, they could outrun German U-boats. Hitler offered a reward and a silver cross to anyone who could sink them, but no one could. After the war, the ships operated as luxury liners for many years.

Poole left Nova Scotia and set out for the Royal Navy base in Scapa Flow, a bay-like body of water located in the Orkney Islands off the north coast of Scotland. Germans surely held a grudge about the area, as it was here that they had to surrender most of their fleet at the end of World War I.

At the very beginning of World War II, in October of 1939, a German U-boat slipped into Scapa Flow. It fired upon and sank the battleship *HMS Royal Oak*, which was at anchor with a crew of over 1,200 aboard. Over 880 crewmen perished. This was fuel for Hitler's propaganda machine right at the start of the war – this was more proof of Nazi superiority, Hitler claimed. To the British, the words "Scapa Flow" evoke emotions similar to those of Americans when reminded of Pearl Harbor.

From Scapa Flow, the *Tuscaloosa* went on to provide fire support – bombardment -- in one of the most famous operations in military history: D-Day. The *Tuscaloosa's* crew suffered no fatalities but bore the psychological scars of fierce warfare. As the ship neared New York, the Statue of Liberty came into view, soaring high into the sky. The emotion of the men when they spotted Lady Liberty was staggering. Men were crying. They couldn't believe they didn't die, didn't get hurt.

Poole and the *Tuscaloosa* saw action in the Pacific too, though not together. Poole was assigned to a new ship after returning from Europe. The *Tuscaloosa* went on to participate in the invasion of Iwo Jima and Okinawa. By war's end, she had earned seven battle stars, four of which were for battles that were critical to the Allied victory.

Poole was assigned to a brand new ship, which was he thought was "something else." The *USS Alaska* was a large cruiser laid down on December 17, 1941, by the New York Shipbuilding Company in Camden, New Jersey. She was launched on August 15, 1943, sponsored by the wife of the governor of the territory of Alaska, and commissioned on June 17, 1944. Grand and majestic, she was "as big as a battleship" Poole thought. Poole was aboard the ship on her last shakedown cruise in the fall of 1944, and then they went through the Panama Canal, over to California and then to war.

At age nineteen, Poole was in charge of about thirty young men as they steamed out across the Pacific to bomb the Japanese (who were a lot scarier than the Germans, in Poole's opinion). Poole and his crew worked on the smokestacks on the deck of the ship, and Poole felt that it was hard to deal with his crew because they were from New York, and he was from Ohio. His crew thought they were tougher than Poole and didn't respect his authority. Poole was so frustrated with them that he was ready to throw the whole bunch of them over the side of the ship. Poole earned his men's deference and respect, however, once they experienced combat.

Their time aboard the *Alaska* included bombardment missions against the heavily defended Japanese homeland. They were getting shot at every day, and the crew realized that Poole was trying to keep them alive. All of Poole's men survived the war.

Petty Officer Poole's story concludes in Chapter 26.

Photograph of Glenn Miller, taken by Photographer De-Belllis in New York in 1943.
Photo Courtesy of the American Music Research Center, Glenn Miller Archive.

Troop Morale,
The USO and Major Glenn Miller's Army Air Forces Band

World War II leaders were well aware of the importance of troop morale and paid special attention to providing entertainment and relaxation for those who served. The USO, or United Services Organizations, was the mainstay of military entertainment during the war. The USO was a civilian volunteer organization formed in 1941 with the approval of President Roosevelt.

With one million volunteers and representatives from Christian, Catholic and Jewish organizations, the USO established over 3,000 clubs all across the country to provide places for troops to relax and have fun. The people who turned their local social clubs into USO clubs did so voluntarily, as a way to help in the war effort. The clubs provided an immeasurable amount of comfort to the homesick troops. Servicemen and women could go to the clubs for formal entertainment or just to drink coffee, and meet new friends and old. Many USOs held informal dances, where the military boys danced with the local girls.

The USO also staged shows in the U.S. and in more than forty foreign countries, on military bases and posts and aboard ships. The most famous Hollywood stars performed in USO shows. as did more than 5,000 lesser-known performers. Seventeen USO performers were killed in the war.

In addition to the USO's shows and clubs, and thanks to a famous, dedicated and talented American bandleader named Glenn Miller, an official Army Air Forces band led by the most popular bandleader in the U.S also provided entertainment for troops. In 1942, the famous bandleader– who, in terms of U.S. popularity, was the World War II equivalent of Bono or the Beatles – asked for and was granted a commission into the Army Air Forces to help entertain the troops.

Dancing was hugely popular during the war years, and the rage was for a new type of music called "swing." Played by orchestras and also known as "big band music," swing was a highly orchestrated jazz spin-off. Teenagers loved its energy, and adults appreciated its strong rhythms and melodies. It took its name from the 1932 hit song It Don't Mean a Thing if it Ain't Got That Swing, *by Duke Ellington.*

In the years leading up to the war, big bands toured the country, playing swing music to packed dancehalls, making recordings and broadcasting on radio shows. The most popular band undoubtedly was the Glenn Miller Orchestra, which had more than fifty top ten recordings from 1940 to 1942, a hit radio series called "Moonlight Serenade" and two movies to its credit. Glenn Miller's hits such as In the Mood, String of Pearls, Chatanooga Choo Choo, Pennsylvania 6-5000 *and* Moonlight Serenade *provided the musical backdrop for the war years.*

Miller was a devoted American patriot. In his late 30's and exempt from the draft, he staged concerts for troops and played at rallies to raise money for war bonds. He eventually requested an Army commission to entertain troops. His request coincided with the launch of a new Army auxiliary unit, called the Army Specialist Corps, or ASC, which trained Miller and others over several months and was then dissolved.

The ASC took top professionals from the civilian entertainment industry and trained them to be in charge of military entertainment programs. In addition to Miller, the ASC included Maurice Evans, who was the premiere Shakespearean actor in the U.S. and John Shubert whose family's theater business established the Broadway theater district in New York City. These ASC officers were not considered to be a part of the regular Army and did not wear regular Army uniforms, but when the program dissolved in November 1942, they were able to join the regular Army with the ranks they held in the ASC.

When the ASC program dissolved, Captain Maurice Evans accepted a commission with the regular Army and went on to coordinate entertainment programs with the USO. Schubert returned to civilian life.

After the ASC program ended, Captain Glenn Miller was named Director of *Bands Training for the Army Air Forces Technical Training Command in 1943 and, at his request, was assigned to form an orchestra. He chose the absolutely best musicians from across the country. He got the top swing musicians as well as the best strings players from symphony orchestras – some would call this cherry-picking – and formed the Army Air Forces Band, which has been described as the best swing band of all time.*

In the spring of 1943, the band got together and began rehearsing at Yale University in New Haven, Connecticut. The band played for the troops in training at Yale, during their marches and for their entertainment. They also played at concerts for the war effort, raising millions of dollars, and they performed in the studio for radio broadcasts. During these broadcasts, Miller encouraged people to help out in the war effort in any way they could.

In a broadcast soon after D-Day, Miller announced that, "Over on the beaches of Normandy our boys have fired the opening guns of the long await-ed drive to liberate the world." In the months following D-Day, in the sum-mer of 1944, just over a year since its formation, the band was sent to En-gland. Miller and his band worked as hard as they could to entertain the troops overseas. In one month alone, they played at thirty-five different bases and in forty broadcasts. In July, Miller was promoted to the rank of Major.

A few months later, the orchestra participated more directly in the war effort. In the fall of 1944, Glenn Miller and his band recorded six shows directed toward German civilians, playing their American swing music and demonstrating how great America was. The studio where they recorded the shows was located on Abbey Road in London and was the same studio where the Beatles would eventually record one of the most famous rock and roll albums ever – Abbey Road.

Soon after Glenn Miller arrived in England, Paris was liberated from German occupation, in August of 1944. After the orchestra finished its re-cordings at the studio on Abbey Road, Miller was ordered to move his band to Paris, to entertain troops there. A big Christmas concert was planned, and the troops stationed in and near Paris could not believe they actually had something to look forward to on another Christmas overseas, far away from home. They knew the war was coming to an end, but there was much more fighting to endure. The Battle of the Bulge was getting underway, it was the beginning of what would be one of the coldest winters on record in Europe, and the Allies still had not invaded the German homeland. Germany was severely weakened, but hundreds of thousands of German troops fought on. Everyone was excited about the Glenn Miller concert.

On December 15, a foggy day, Miller boarded a military transport plane headed to France to help set up for the Christmas concert. The band would arrive several days later. Miller's plane went missing over the English Channel. It was never found. Ten days later, the Army Air Forces announced that Glenn Miller had become another casualty of World War II. The band played the Paris Christmas concert, without him, to thousands of troops grieving yet another war loss.

Miller earned the Bronze Star Medal, the World War II Victory Medal, the American Campaign Medal, the European, African and Middle Eastern Campaign Medal and the Marksman Badge with Carbine and Pistol Bars.

This photograph, dated February 9, 1945, shows troops of the U.S. 7th Armored Division advancing through Belgium in the Battle of the Bulge. Photograph number 65640, courtesy of the Franklin D. Roosevelt Presidential Library and Museum.

14

*The Battle of the Bulge, the Siegfried Line and the Service
of Technical Sergeant William Burrus, U.S. Army*

During the summer following D-Day, in 1944, the Allies drove the Germans out of much of Europe and back toward Germany. By September, the Allies were preparing for the end of the war, when they would charge into the German homeland. Once in Germany, the Allies would take down German troops and knock out the country's infrastructure to the point where Germany could fight no more. This was the big picture of how the Allies would end the war, defeating Hitler. For the Allied infantrymen, however, there was no big picture.

The infantrymen fought on foot, one bullet at a time. They marched or were trucked to the edge of a town, village or city that German soldiers controlled and were ordered to "attack," "patrol" or "take" the place. They sometimes did not even know where they were, and that didn't really matter. With their guns in their hands and their buddies by their sides, these sharpshooters ran straight into enemy territory, fighting man to man, across German-occupied Europe and into Germany itself. They fought until the war was won. Casualties were so high that some men reported that they did not want to be friendly with the replacement troops who joined them on the frontlines because they couldn't bear to lose another friend.

In addition to his gun, each foot soldier carried a backpack, a bedroll, a ration of food and a folding shovel, so he could dig himself a foxhole in the ground to stay in during the fighting. Technical Sergeant William Burrus served as a rifleman in the 87th Infantry Division of General Patton's Third

Army – he was one of these men on the frontlines of the war. He marched and fought his way through France, Belgium and Luxembourg in the Rhineland Campaign and the Battle of the Bulge and across Germany until Hitler was defeated. The infantrymen fought, slept and ate in the rain and snow throughout one of the most frigid European winters on record.

Growing up, Burrus did not seem to be headed toward serving on the frontlines of war. Born in Birmingham, Alabama, in 1926, he was the baby in his family, with two older sisters and a brother. Burrus enjoyed a happy childhood. He was raised in a nice, modest home, and his father had a good job as a railroad yardmaster during the Great Depression. His maternal grandfather owned racehorses, and his parents both liked to ride. His family was returning home to Birmingham from a visit with relatives on his father's side of the family in St. Louis, Missouri, in December 1941, when Japan bombed Pearl Harbor. Burrus didn't think much about the attack – he was just fifteen years old at the time. He was enjoying high school where he played in the band as a drum major and was a cheerleader for the football team.

Three years after Pearl Harbor, Burrus registered for the draft, on his eighteenth birthday. It was late in the war, and the U.S. needed troops fast. Burrus was called up to serve pretty quickly, pulled out of high school before graduating, and sent to basic training in Florida. There, the Army discovered that he was good with a gun. Burrus had been raised a strict Catholic and had never used a hand arm of any type before. He had never even had a BB gun. His talent was natural. At training, he was proud of his proficiency on the M-1 rifle and pleased that he was known as a "sharpshooter," not realizing that this meant that he would be on the front lines.

Burrus was shipped out to war on November 4, 1944, landed in England one week later, and by November 28, he was marching across France with his rifle and gear. He marched for six weeks straight once. He joined up with the 87th Infantry, which was newly formed and nicknamed the Golden Acorn Division. Burrus began fighting in December, in the Saar region of France, a geographically key area that became an Allied protectorate after the war. From here, Burrus and his fellow survivors in the 87th would go on to fight steadily for more than five months, not even able to take a bath or change clothes for the most part.

Although everyone knew the war was ending, there was still a lot of fighting to do. The German army and infrastructure had been severely weakened throughout years of warfare, but hundreds of thousands of German soldiers still fought, and they were determined to fiercely protect their homeland. The Germans made this point clear on December 16, 1944, about a week after Burrus began combat.

At this time in the war, Eisenhower had developed a long front of Allied forces to the west of Germany as a part of the Rhineland Campaign. The Allies were advancing toward the Rhine River and were set to cross the river at three points, which would take them strongly into the German homeland. In September of 1944, however, Eisenhower acknowledged that the Allies would not be able to win the war by the end of the year and would have to fight on through the winter. The Allies were short on fuel, equipment and men, partly because they were bringing everything in from the beaches of Normandy, which were rough and unsheltered and far from the front. Eisenhower believed that the German Army was still strong. The Germans were sure to lose the war, but they would go down fighting.

On December 15, Allied intelligence reported no activity on the long, western front. The next morning brought a colossal surprise – more than 200,000 German troops armed with nearly 3,000 tanks and guns rolled across sixty miles of the Allied front in a huge attack, soon followed by two more waves of troops and tanks. This surprise attack took place along the Belgian-Luxembourg-German border, in the Ardennes Forest. Allied communication lines were hit, and commanders had to scramble to respond to the attack.

Hitler had been planning this since D-Day, and he gave it all he had. On December 17, the Germans committed atrocities when an armored assault unit attacked Malmedy, Belgium, and German troops murdered more than 300 U.S. prisoners of war and more than 100 unarmed Belgian civilians. In January, the Germans launched their last major attack of the war in the Alsace region of France. Allied troops referred to the officially- named "Ardennes-Alsace Campaign" as the "Battle of the Bulge," because the German offensive made a bulge on the map of the long Allied western front.

The Battle of the Bulge was beginning to wind down when Burrus arrived at the front. The 87th Infantry left the Saar region in France and travelled over 100 miles in open cars in the freezing cold to Belgium in late December to fight near the town of Bastogne, in the south side of the "bulge," where the 101st U.S. Airborne Division was under siege. They fought there in bitter wintry weather. A storm called a "Russian High" had brought snow and extreme cold to the area on December 23, marking the beginning of what would be an excessively cold and snowy winter.

The Germans hit U.S troops with artillery, machine guns, tanks and automatic weapons. By the end of January, the Allies had beaten the Germans back, but the cost was high. More than 800,000 Allied troops fought in the Battle of the Bulge, and Allied casualties numbered almost 100,000. Tens of thousands of men were hospitalized for frostbite, trench foot and other weather-related injuries.

Burrus' next challenge was to help take Germany's famous Siegfried Line, an enormous line of fortifications along the western border of Germany, much touted by Hitler's propaganda as an un-passable line of defense. The strongest part of the line was where Burrus and the rest of the 87th crossed, along the Saar River between the Mosell and Rhine Rivers. Here, German soldiers, many of them recently conscripted old men and young boys, manned interconnected concrete guard huts or "pillboxes." The Siegfried Line was also fortified with mines and obstacles such as "dragon's teeth" – steel-reinforced concrete spears that stuck up out of the ground like enormous, crooked teeth. By the end of February, the 87th had made it across the line. Burrus was scared to death most of the time, but he followed orders. Many troops were killed and wounded by the mines and the fire from the pillboxes. A U.S. Army report on the work of the Third and Seventh Armies in crossing the Siegfried Line described "the incredible bravery and self-sacrifice American soldiers once more exhibited in the face of the determined German defenses."

After crossing the Siegfried Line, the 87th crossed the Moselle River into the Saar-Palatinate region, an area between the Moselle, Saar and Rhine Rivers. Burrus was surprised that crossing the Moselle was not too tough, but the Germans attacked them violently on the other side. Burrus and the others fought on streets, along fences, dodging sniper fire and automatic fire. They fought from house to house, going through basements and shooting from attics.

By the middle of March, the 87th had penetrated and seized Koblenz, the capital of the Rhineland region. It was a heavily defended city with a population of around 100,000. Later that month, the VIII Corps Headquarters of the U.S. Army commended the division for its "Can Do" attitude and for its work: "The most recent mission of forcing a crossing of the Moselle River, capturing Koblenz, and clearing the enemy from the area … was a difficult one made easy by the hard work and superior cooperation by all members…. The 87th Division no longer can be considered inexperienced and unseasoned. The division now takes rank with other fine, experienced combat organizations in the U.S. Army."

The Allies' next step was to cross the mighty Rhine River, the second largest river in Europe, into Germany. Eisenhower had planned to have British forces in the north cross the Rhine first, but when he saw how successfully Patton's Third Army had performed in the south, he decided to give the Third Army the prize of crossing into Germany first.

Burrus was in the first wave of the 87th crossing the Rhine River. There were ten of them in the boat and it was cold. They carried food because they didn't know how long they would be out fighting on their own on the front line. It might be days before their company caught up with them. Burrus was assigned to carry ammunition for M-1 rocket launchers. Known as bazookas, these rocket launchers were about the size of a rifle and an infantryman's best weapon against a German tank. He carried the miniature rockets by strapping them around his body. They were very heavy, and he knew that he would drown if he fell into the water.

Burrus was in one of about thirty small boats crossing the Rhine. Burrus and the others had been told that it would be a surprise attack, but the Germans were there and ready for them. The men got into their boats and suddenly saw white, then yellow, and then red flares. The Germans lit up the water so they could see the men and then they started firing at them. The firing was fierce. The 87th crossed in a gorge between 300-foot tall mountains. Germans were stationed high on the mountainsides on the other side of the river. They fired directly down upon the men in the boats using 16-foot-barreled anti-tank guns, mortar shells and more. Many men were hit, and the sounds of screaming filled the air.

Burrus' sergeant, George Craig, told them to just keep their heads down and keep paddling. Craig was a great leader, and his encouragement and leadership helped them survive the crossing. Burrus made it across the river through the heavy fire and got out of the boat. He lay on the bank for a while, saying the rosary and promising to say it every day for the rest of his life.

The 87th fought throughout the day. People were shooting at them from trees and houses, but they secured the area by night. Once the engineers installed bridges across the river, they could bring the tanks in.

Burrus' unit earned a Presidential Unit Citation for crossing in that first wave into heavy enemy fire. The citation reads in part as follows:

The First Battalion, 347th Infantry Regiment, 87th Infantry Division, distinguished itself by conspicuous heroism and exemplary teamwork during the crossing of the Rhine River, Germany, in the early morning of 25 March 1945....In the face of heavy fire, the first assault wave, without hesitation, completed the crossing and engaged the enemy on the east shore. As each wave hit the east shore they quickly reorganized and bitterly fought their way forward in spite of heavy enemy defenses....It was discovered later that the enemy had been ordered to hold this particular ground at all costs....The gallant performance of this unit and the conspicuous heroism and courageous determination of each member are in keeping with the highest traditions of the military service.

The morning after crossing the Rhine, the 87th began its drive against the enemy into the heart of Germany. Over the next month, the 87th fought through more than 100 miles of enemy territory. Burrus was surprised that the Germans could speak English as well as he could. There were rumors of Germans wearing U.S. military uniforms and thereby getting close in to Allied forces to make a kill.

The Germans managed to trap Burrus and some other soldiers in a forest at one point. The boys crouched in the woods under mortar fire and dodged the tree branches that thundered to the ground in the firestorm. Lots of kids got killed there. Burrus tried not to get too close emotionally to his fellow soldiers because of all the death. His training had been terrific, very tough, but he realized that you had to have lots of luck over there.

Sometimes the fighting was from house to house, as the infantrymen made sure to find any German soldiers in hiding. Once, as he walked through a home he thought was empty, Burrus suddenly came upon a woman standing with a little girl. He was very startled. The little girl gave him an apple, a gesture that touched his heart. As he left the house, he saw a Catholic crucifix on the wall and enjoyed the feeling of having connected with someone who shared his religious faith. His faith was keeping him strong.

Sergeant Burrus' story concludes in Chapter 24.

U.S. troops crossing the Siegfried Line into Germany in 1945.
Photo courtesy of the U.S. National Archives, number 208-YE-193.

A 1942 poster featuring a Tuskegee Airman.
Photo courtesy of the FDR Library Museum.
Object Number MO 2005.13.36.192.1.

15

Fighter Pilots, The Tuskegee Airmen
And the Service of Lt. Colonel Harry D. Stewart, Jr.,
U.S. Army Air Forces

As a child, Harry Stewart dreamed of flying. Born in 1924, in Newport News, Virginia, he moved with his family at age two to the Borough of Queens in New York City, near North Beach Airfield. Stewart watched the planes land and take off – half commercial flights and half Army – at the small airfield that would become LaGuardia Airport. His young dreams of flying came true. Stewart served in World War II as a fighter pilot, flying an incredible forty-three bomber escort missions in the P-51 Mustang, a single-seat fighter. He engaged frequently in the extremely dangerous action known as aerial combat or "dogfighting" – where two planes attack each other directly. Stewart was credited with personally shooting down three German FW-190s in a dogfight following a bombing mission over Austria.

Stewart served in the war as a member of the Tuskegee Airmen, a segregated Army Air Forces unit staffed by African-American pilots, crews and support personnel. Until the Tuskegee Airmen proved them wrong, many people – both military and civilian – believed that blacks and other minorities were incapable of piloting a plane and incapable of serving in combat, even though black people and other minorities have served with distinction in combat roles in the U.S. military in every U.S. war, including the Revolutionary War.

The Army Air Forces did not train blacks to be pilots until it was forced to do so just prior to World War II, arguing that it would be too logistically complicated to have black pilots because blacks had to live and work separately from whites or work in subservient roles to whites – segregation was the rule because the military reflected the civilian culture. The Army Air Forces also pointed to official policy from World War I stating that black people were unfit to be pilots.

By serving in World War II with the utmost talent, dedication and bravery, Stewart and his fellow Tuskegee Airmen showed that black people and other minorities ought to serve equally with white people in the U.S. Armed Forces and paved the way for desegregation of the military.

Stewart's odyssey began at age seventeen, when he sat for the Army's tough cadet aviation examination and passed the test. When he turned eighteen, the Air Corps sent him a letter with his assignment as a pre-aviation cadet. Stewart did his basic training at Keesler Air Force base in Biloxi, Mississippi, and then was sent for flight training at the Tuskegee Institute, an all black college in Tuskegee, Alabama.

At the time, all-black schools like Tuskegee were common in the U.S. because until long after the war – until after the Civil Rights Movement of the 1960's – the U.S. was a racially segregated country. After slavery was abolished in the 1860's, some people fought for equal treatment of the newly freed slaves, but they were unsuccessful – many people thought that blacks were inferior to whites and should be treated as such. Then, in 1896, the U.S. Supreme Court ruled that providing "separate but equal" accommodations for blacks was lawful, making segregation legal – a government entity or a business could lawfully exclude blacks and other minorities from anything and everything: jobs, housing, schools, a seat on a bus or a ticket to a movie. Black people were second-class citizens in most areas of American life, and the military was no exception.

The military reflected the civilian culture. Throughout the U.S., blacks and whites lived and worked apart from each other, and where they did mix, blacks were in subservient roles. Black people had their own neighborhoods, stores, schools, doctors, lawyers, etc. Where blacks and whites did work together, blacks had the menial jobs. The Army followed suit, and at the beginning of World War II, a few all-black Army units existed, but they were supply and construction units and were commanded by white officers.

Black people and some others protested this arrangement and argued that blacks should have more opportunities in the Army and should be allowed to fly. These protests resulted in the passage of Public Law 18, in 1939, which required that the Army Air Corps create training programs for blacks at black colleges, just as whites trained for certain Army jobs at white colleges. The Army complied with the new law, but many people, military and civilian, thought it was a bad idea. Many thought that training black people to fly, the "Tuskegee Experiment," as some called it, would fail.

In 1941, the Army instituted flight training for black cadets at the Tuskegee Institute, now Tuskegee University, in Tuskegee, Alabama. Eventually, almost one thousand black aviation cadets earned their pilot's wings at Tuskegee. For every pilot who graduated, there were ten to twelve people in support – doctors, drivers, nurses, and so on. That means there were 10,000 to 12,000 people who could say they were Tuskegee Airmen. Stewart believed that all these people deserved credit for being Tuskegee Airmen as well, and that it wasn't quite right that the pilots seemed to get all the credit for the program. Another misconception about the Tuskegee Air Force base was that everyone there was African-American. Especially early on, before blacks had been through training, white officers and instructors worked at Tuskegee and most were very supportive of the program.

Tuskegee was chosen in part because it already had a civilian flying program, started by one of the first black pilots in the country, the self-taught Charles Alfred ("Chief") Anderson. In the spring of 1941, First Lady Eleanor Roosevelt visited the Tuskegee Institute, and Anderson took her for a ride in a biplane. The First Lady wrote very favorably about the school, her ride with Anderson and Tuskegee's pilot training program in her syndicated newspaper column, "My Day" on April 1, 1941, which was good publicity for the program – Tuskegee was trying to change people's conceptions of black people's intelligence and capabilities.

In order to pilot a plane in the military, a person must have perfect vision, a natural, inherent talent for operating the plane's controls and maneuvering through the air, and excellent scores in flight school, none of which is easy to do. Stewart trained to fly the P-51 Mustang, a single-seat fighter, which meant that he would fly his missions as the sole person aboard his plane. As his training manual explained, "being a first-rate fighter pilot means being not only a pilot, but a whole crew – pilot, navigator, gunner, bombardier, and radio operator – all rolled into one."

Stewart's initial training consisted of half days of classroom work in physics, navigation, radio and other subjects. The other half of the day was spent in the air. As with all Air Corps cadet training, Tuskegee cadets were tested after each level of training, and those who did not make the grade were dismissed from the program and reassigned to another job in the Army. After sixty hours of flight time on the P-13 primary trainer, successful cadets moved onto a more complicated plane, the BT-13, the basic trainer.

The cadets learned to use flight "checklists" – standardized operating procedures for various aspects of flying a particular plane (and the origin of the term "flying by the book"). They learned ground operations, takeoffs, turns, climbs, descents and landings. Stewart had a delightful time, and what eighteen year-old aviation buff would not have? They learned how to do stalls and spins, acrobatic maneuvers, parachute landings, bailouts (emergency parachuting), formation flying, night flying and instrument flying. Stewart loved every minute of it.

Stewart successfully completed the primary and basic levels and was promoted to sixty hours of advanced training on the AT-6, which was a more maneuverable and technologically advanced plane than the other trainers and more like the plane he would fly in the war. In addition to flight training, Stewart and the other cadets received classroom instruction in advanced navigation, armament, gunnery, air fighting techniques and tactics, and flight maintenance and engineering. Being a fighter pilot was a big job.

Stewart graduated from Tuskegee's Aviation Cadet program and was awarded his pilot's wings and a commission as a second lieutenant in the United States Army Air Force. He was nineteen years old and as happy as a lark at his achievements. It was June of 1944, and Stewart went home to see his family on a ten-day leave before final training and shipping out to Europe.

After his leave, Stewart was sent to the Walterboro Army Airfield base in Walterboro, South Carolina, for advanced individual air combat training, or as the guys called it, "fighter tactics." One day in the air, he crossed paths with another plane, and they engaged in mock warfare, also known as "aircraft tag." The other pilot was very accomplished and outmaneuvered Stewart. Afterward, they landed next to each other. He looked over at the pilot, and there was a woman, removing her helmet while flaming red hair fell to her shoulders. She was a WASP! Stewart was impressed and humbled by how well she could fly.

At the height of its workload, the Women Airforce Service Pilots (WASP) program ferried over half the planes in the U.S. from factories to bases and between bases. They flew bombers and fighters, and Stewart considered them to be quite a distinguished group. The women were civilians and did not receive military benefits at the time, but they led the way for women to join the U.S. Air Force.

After about three months of training, seven days a week, Stewart headed to war. He left from Norfolk, Virginia, on a liberty ship, one of thousands of small ships used to transport troops during the war. He traveled in a convoy with about nineteen other ships. As they neared Europe, the ships began to go their separate ways to the various ports to which they were headed. Stewart's ship went to Italy alone. The men felt scared and lonely out there by themselves, especially knowing the U-boats could torpedo them at any time. They felt very lucky when they arrived unharmed.

The first pilots who trained at Tuskegee formed the first all-black flying unit in the U.S. military, eventually called the 99th Fighter Squadron. The 99th was attached to various white fighter groups but not formally assigned to any. In P-40 fighters, the 99th flew patrol missions in North Africa beginning in April of 1943. The 99th went on to enemy-occupied Sicily and Italy, in P-39, P-40 and P-47 fighters, attacking strategic targets, providing air cover for Allied ground forces and earning two Distinguished Unit Citations. These men were proving the critics of Tuskegee wrong.

As more men trained at Tuskegee, the number of black pilots grew. In early 1944, the 332nd all-black Fighter Group was formed, as a part of the 15th Air Force. The Group consisted of the 100th, 301st and 302nd Fighter Squadrons as well as the 99th Fighter Squadron, which formally joined the 332nd Fighter Group in Italy in 1944. For a while, the 332nd Fighter Group carried out missions similar to those of the 99th Fighter Squadron, but soon its missions changed.

The Tuskegee Airmen started flying escort in long-range, heavy bombardment missions deep into enemy territory in German-occupied Europe. They flew red-tailed P-51 Mustangs and showed once and for all that blacks could fly with distinction in combat missions.

Stewart was assigned to the 301st Fighter Squadron and arrived in Italy in January of 1945. His squadron's base was in Ramitelli, right on the Adriatic Coast, just above the "heel" of Italy. Stewart flew forty-three bomber escort missions in his red-tailed Mustang.

For Stewart, flying on a long-range bombing mission, hours and hours of flying alone, was the most boring thing in the world – except for the moments of sheer terror. Stewart's plane was loaded for action. He had six .50 caliber M2 machine guns, three under each wing, with a total ammunition capacity of 1,880 rounds. He also carried ten self-propelled rockets, five under each wing, and bomb racks for up to 1,000 pounds of stores. His Mustang Pilot's Manual had explained that a fighter is basically a flying gun platform. The Mustang was the first plane designed specifically for World War II. It was a beautiful aircraft and the most aerodynamically perfect pursuit plane in existence. The pilots loved their Mustangs.

Early in the morning on April 1, 1945, Stewart climbed into his Mustang and prepared for his missions that day: to escort bombers in a long-range, strategic bombing mission over Bruck, Austria, deep into enemy territory, and to then conduct a fighter sweep of Linz, Austria, looking for enemy aircraft and certain enemy targets, such as factories, to destroy. Twenty-seven planes – B-24 bombers of the 47th Bombardment Wing escorted by Tuskegee Airmen in their P-51 fighters -- stormed out of their base in Italy and headed to bomb the St. Polten marshaling yard, a key military railroad site in Bruck, six-hundred miles away. It was Easter Sunday.

After the bombers had dropped their bombs over their targets and headed back toward Italy, Stewart and six other fighters looked for other enemy targets. They ran into a squadron of German fighters, *Focke-Wulf*-190s, and had a dogfight – basically a gunfight between two people who are flying airplanes. Stewart shot down two enemy planes. A third German fighter was shooting at Stewart aggressively. Stewart outmaneuvered him, and down the German went. The Air Force awarded Stewart the Distinguished Flying Cross for shooting down three German *Focke-Wulf*-190s that day.

Colonel Stewart's story concludes in Chapter 24.

Seabees Recruiting Poster. Photo courtesy of the U.S. Navy.

16

The Naval Construction Battalions, the Seabees
And the Service of Petty Officer Buck Lord, U.S. Navy

It is widely believed that the U.S. prevailed in the war due to its overwhelming production of supplies and number of well-trained troops. Construction projects were also key. Bridges, airstrips, hospitals and many other structures must be built in order to carry out war. In January of 1942, the U.S. Navy began to form a Naval Construction Regiment so that construction crews and engineers could carry arms and defend themselves as they engaged in the perilous work of wartime construction. The regiment consisted of three Construction Battalions and took its name from the initials of the words "Construction" and "Battalions." The "Seabees'" official motto is the Latin-English phrase, "Construimus, Batuimus –- We Build, We Fight."

More than 300,000 men from more than sixty skilled trades served with the Seabees, including those who had worked on major construction projects like the Boulder Dam and those who had built ships, highways and skyscrapers. The Seabees were legendary for their ingenuity and almost uncanny ability to build anything, anywhere, with whatever tools and equipment were available. The first Seabees were older than the average military recruits – many were in their thirties or forties or even older – and they earned a reputation for being a bit more independent and feisty than a typical, young inductee just out of high school. The Seabees served with distinction in the Pacific and European Theaters, and their work in the Pacific has been described as unparalleled in the history of wartime construction.

The Seabees built more than one hundred major airstrips, more than four hundred piers, thousands of warehouses, hospitals for more than 60,000 patients and housing for 1.5 million troops. During the course of the war, more than three hundred Seabees were killed by the enemy, more than five hundred were killed in construction accidents, and more than two thousand Seabees were awarded the Purple Heart. For their valor, members of the Seabees earned thirty-three Silver Star Medals and five Navy Crosses.

Petty Officer Buck Lord served in the 301st Harbor Reclamation Battalion of the Seabees and was stationed in Guam, arriving just as the U.S. was defeating the Japanese there and "mopping up" began to get underway. Wartime mopping up is the very dangerous period after official battle ends when the victors have to ensure that stragglers from the enemy troops are removed from the area. These stragglers were often snipers who wanted to continue to fight. During the last days of battle, the mopping up, and for several months afterward, Lord helped build the Apra Harbor and Glass Breakwater in Guam, considered to be the largest Seabee project of the war and comparable in scope to the building of the Panama Canal.

Growing up, Lord had never imagined that he would find himself one day working on an enormous wartime construction project in the Pacific Ocean. He was born in 1922, on a small family farm about thirty miles outside of Dallas, Texas. His family grew corn and oats to feed their barn animals and planted cotton as a money crop. The youngest of seven children, Lord attended an old-fashioned, one-room school, where grades one through seven were all taught together, and his eldest sister was his teacher there for a few years. He graduated from high school at age sixteen in the 11th grade, as there was no 12th grade at the time, took a job at the Haggar Pants Company, and then married his girlfriend, Frankie, when he was nineteen and she was twenty years old. She worked at Haggar too.

When the war began, the factory started to manufacture military uniforms. Lord registered for the draft but was eligible for a deferment since his work was considered to be necessary to the national defense program. Lord and his wife had married shortly after the U.S. entered the war, and over the months he watched his friends get drafted. He and Frankie talked it over and decided that he should serve too. It didn't feel right not to. He enlisted in the Navy in 1943 in Fort Worth, Texas, and was sent to Seabees training in Williamsburg, Virginia. After training, he was sent to Guam.

Japan had invaded Guam on December 10, 1941. The people of Guam endured brutal, often horrific, treatment under Japanese rule. People were raped, beheaded, tortured and executed in mass, among other atrocities. Guam is the largest island in Micronesia and has been a territory of the U.S. since the Spanish-American War.

On July 21, 1944, the U.S. Marines landed on Guam and fierce fighting ensued. U.S. troops fought the Japanese for three weeks, and on August 10, the Japanese surrendered the island. Lord arrived later that month. After the surrender many Japanese soldiers – stragglers – continued to fight, not wanting to surrender. They hid in the jungle and looked for U.S troops to take out with sniper fire. Lord had arrived in a dangerous place.

Lord helped dredge the Apra Harbor, a natural, deep harbor on the western side of Guam. It is located close to the Mariana Trench, which is one of the deepest parts of ocean in the world. Lord and his fellow Seabees used dynamite to break up the underwater coral and then removed the rubble they had created. They took the coral that they dredged up and made an island. That island, part of which was naturally made, is known as the Glass Breakwater and is located in the northern part of the harbor. It was dangerous work.

On one occasion, two of Lord's buddies were killed when the dynamite they were using went off accidentally. One of them had five children at home, and the other had three children. The tough Seabees out in the hot Pacific sympathized with the men's families. One of the guys had a sword that had belonged to a Japanese officer. He auctioned it off and sent the money to the families of the men who were killed.

Lord and his fellow Seabees worked hard on Guam. The island is strategically located in the Micronesian Islands near Japan, so it would serve as the advance headquarters for the U.S. Pacific Fleet, an airbase for U.S. heavy bombers and other planes, and a major war supply center. Taking back Guam was key to Allied success in the Pacific. The B-29 Superfortresses would be based in Guam, and these were the planes that would defeat Japan.

Petty Officer Lord's story concludes in Chapter 24.

*Photograph of Amelia Earhart courtesy of the
National Aeronautics and Space Administration.*

The Golden Age of Aviation

The years between the two world wars have been called the "Golden Age of Aviation." As World War II approached, Americans were fascinated with flying. Most people went to the movies at least once a week (for a quarter or a dime – a movie ticket didn't cost much during the Depression), and many movies featured flying and air combat. Moviegoers snacked on the popcorn and candy apples made at the theaters as well as the new factory-made candies like Baby Ruth bars. Hell's Angels, Only Angels Have Wings *and other films by director Howard Hawks depicted aviators as glamorous, brave men facing danger in the sky.*

Ordinary men and women got their pilot's licenses and joined flying clubs or just read about aviation races, contests, and stunts in the newspaper. Top aviators were celebrities. The glamorous Charles Lindbergh, who grew up in Minnesota, was famous around the world for his solo flight across the Atlantic Ocean. Amelia Earhart was the most famous female aviator in the 1930's. This beautiful woman from Kansas was the first person to fly solo across both the Atlantic and Pacific Oceans. Her disappearance in her plane over the Pacific Ocean in 1937 was a great mystery and another amazing aviation story that Americans followed with rapt attention. Americans' romance with flying, however, would be another casualty of World War II. During the war, aviation firmly established itself as an important military force. For people at home reading about the war and seeing photographs of bombed-out, devastated cities around the world, aviation no longer seemed as exciting or glamorous.

U.S Air Force photograph of the B-29 Superfortress, named Bockscar, which dropped the second atomic bomb on Japan, on August 9, 1945.

17

The Tokyo Air Raid and the Service of Staff Sergeant Edwin Holopainen, U.S. Army Air Forces

Edwin Holopainen was born in 1926 near the town of Hubbardtston, in central Massachusetts. His parents had emigrated from Finland in the early 1900's, a time when many Finns moved to central Massachusetts to work farms, and Holopainen grew up helping out on his family's dairy farm. The nearby town of Gardner had a small airfield, and sometimes for fun, families in the area would pack picnic lunches, drive over to the airfield and watch the planes land and take off, a very pleasant way to enjoy a sunny day.

The idea of flying was appealing to small-town boys like Holopainen, who was fifteen years old when Japan attacked Pearl Harbor. When the U.S. entered the war, everyone talked about what they were going to do to help in the war effort. Most boys would of course serve in the military, so Holopainen and his buddies talked about which military branches they preferred. Holopainen thought that he would like to be in the Army Air Forces so that he could fly.

Holopainen would turn eighteen on January 31, 1944, and the plan for his birthday – like that of every American boy turning eighteen during the war – was to register with the local draft board, as required by law, and wait to be drafted into whatever branch the government placed him in.

Holopainen had a different idea though. If he enlisted, he could choose the branch he wanted and avoid the possibility of getting drafted into the infantry. This meant he would have to quit high school, but it was worth it to him. He knew he did not want to march with the infantry through the war. He wanted to fly. His parents were proud of their American-born son who wanted to serve their adoptive country in the Army Air Forces. On his eighteenth birthday, Holopainen walked into the AAF recruiting station local enlistment office, in Springfield, Massachusetts, instead of into the local draft board office, and joined the Army Air Forces. His plan worked perfectly, although he would soon see the very dangerous side of aviation.

Holopainen became an airman, and remarkably, his first mission in the war was as a part of one of the most massive and controversial bombing missions in the history of warfare – the Tokyo Air Raid of March 10, 1945. By most accounts, this attack was more deadly than the dropping of the atomic bombs. More than sixteen square miles of Tokyo were leveled by firebombing in the raid and more than 100,000 people were killed, most of them civilians. Tens of thousands of people were severely injured, and hundreds of thousands were left homeless. It was the first of many devastating firebombing missions over Japan, meant to bring Japan to its knees and surrender.

General Curtis LeMay led the firebombing campaign over Japan and strongly believed that the use of massive force such as this saves lives for both sides in the long run, by shortening the length of war. Holopainen had gotten himself into ferocious warfare, starting with his very first mission. More than half the men in his squadron did not survive their service in the Pacific.

After he enlisted, Holopainen's elementary school held a send-off for him, as it did for all the boys going to war. The school band played patriotic songs, people cried, and the boys who were celebrated felt very important. Next, Holopainen was off to basic training in Greensboro, North Carolina. The training was quite rigorous, and living in a barracks away from home took some getting used to, but Holopainen enjoyed the novelty of it all. The base was in the heart of downtown, so when they earned leave, Holopainen and the other boys could amble around the city in their new uniforms, feeling a bit conspicuous. The boys went to USO clubs and met local girls. They sometimes ate dinner at people's homes because hundreds of families in the area volunteered to entertain the boys going through basic training. The adults in these families were of the generation that had lived through World War I, and they understood what these boys were about to go through.

Holopainen was tested and qualified for gunnery school, in Panama City, Florida. This meant he would be in the air, in combat, as opposed to being a part of the ground crews who maintained the planes. The ground crews often did not want to be friendly with the airmen for the sad reason that so many of them died in the air. At age eighteen, though, Holopainen was excited to be in the aircrew. He was to be a tail gunner on a B-29 Superfortress, the most technologically advanced bomber in the sky. He would sit alone in a compartment at the rear of the plane and shoot .50 caliber machine guns at enemy planes.

After learning how to shoot and operate various types of guns, Holopainen was sent to the B-29 training base in Pratt, Kansas. It was August of 1944, and he had been training for several months, with a three-week break midway through for a quick trip home. Now he would be assigned to his plane and to his aircrew. Holopainen was thrilled with his plane, the state-of-the-art, Boeing B-29 Superfortress. It was brand new, right from the factory. Holopainen thought it was a very modern piece of machinery.

Holopainen and the ten other crewmembers on his plane trained together in Kansas for six months, from August of 1944 until February of 1945. By this time, they worked perfectly together as a team and were ready to head for war.

The crew flew the plane from Kansas to Guam, where they were stationed. It was a very long journey, about 11,000 miles, and the plane was not built for comfort. They were in the air for about thirty-two hours, over several days, and stopped for fuel and sleep in places like California, Hawaii and the Johnston Atoll in the Pacific. Holopainen had never seen places like these, except in the movies. Ground crews serviced the plane at these stops, and while it felt uneasy at first to have strangers working on their plane, the aircrew quickly realized that these ground crews were expert mechanics and had ample supplies for making the necessary services and repairs on their B-29 over its long journey.

When Holopainen and his crew stepped out of their plane onto Guam, the heat hit them like a body blow, and within minutes they were drenched in sweat. Getting used to the terrible heat and to cooling down with only warm water to drink took about two or three weeks.

By the time Holopainen arrived in Guam, seven months after its liberation, the U.S. was deep into massive construction projects on the island, and the place was bustling with work. Roads were jammed with military vehicles. Stacked along the sides of the roads were pile after pile of equipment

and construction materials. The Seabees had to clear dense jungle to establish building sites. Aesthetics were obviously not a priority, so the coconut
trees and jungle grasses they ripped out when clearing the land were not
hauled away but simply bulldozed to the sides of the clearings. Holopainen
and the other new guys stared at the huge piles of raw-cut coconut trees and
jungle grasses that were taller than a man. Beyond the debris lay more jungle. Holopainen had not expected Guam to be such a busy, hectic place.

After a couple of weeks, Holopainen and the other newly arrived men
didn't look like newcomers anymore. They had the same amateur haircuts
and were as tanned and dirty looking as everyone else. Showers were makeshift, soap was not plentiful, and the red jungle dirt and dust dyed clothes,
bedding, tents and just about everything else on the island a rusty red color.

North Field Air Base had been established, but Holopainen and the other
newcomers had to build Quonset huts to live in, sleeping in tents until they
were finished. Each metal hut held about eighteen to twenty men and shel-
tered them for the most part from the giant lizards, the toads, the bats and the
rats that seemed to be everywhere.

Holopainen and his crew cleaned and inspected their plane and flew some
orientation missions. They met the other men, got tips on adapting to their
primitive new environment, and were shown some of the entertainment the
guys had set up – radios for listening to music from the military radio station, a makeshift craps table and rat-shooting contests. Just about everyone
was friendly and jovial. Holopainen got himself settled into his strange new
home, anxious about how his missions would go. He wondered if he would
survive.

North Field Air Base was large and efficient, and early in the morning on
March 9, 1945, ground crews began preparing the aircraft for the enormous
mission that would begin that night as the planes took off for Tokyo. The
ground crews loaded bombs, refueled the planes' tanks, and checked and
tested the planes' equipment. Holopainen and the other airmen were called
to receive their briefings on the mission. The more experienced airmen figured that LeMay would have to employ a new strategy soon, because the
much-touted B-29s had not been performing well. Too many planes had been
lost, and they were not hitting their targets with sufficient accuracy.

As the briefing began, senior officers described the mission. It was defi-
nitely based on a different strategy. More than 300 B-29 Superfortresses –

each over 100 feet long and each weighing more than 140,000 pounds when loaded – were going to fly over an industrial and residential area of Tokyo and drop several tons of firebombs *each* on four targets. The firebombs were M-69s cluster bombs – each cluster would cause thirty-eight streams of intense fires, each stream one hundred feet long, among the wooden buildings that crowded Tokyo. The walls of fire caused by the bombs would sweep together and create an ocean of fire on the ground. Rivers would boil, and tornadoes made of fire would tear through the streets. Industrial Tokyo would become a giant incinerator.

While trying to comprehend the enormity of the mission and its impact on the civilians there, the airmen received a shock. The senior officers informed them that they would be flying into Tokyo at only 5,000 to 10,000 feet off the ground, so they would be closer to their targets. This was unbelievable. They usually flew at 20,000 to 30,000 feet. The airmen understood that LeMay had to change strategy. They knew he expected nothing but heroism from his men in battle. But this seemed to be a suicide mission.

The stunned airmen listened to the briefing and tried not lose their tempers. They tried not to panic. Afterwards, chaplains held religious services, and crowds of airmen poured in to pray and receive blessings. They prayed for their lives. Many prayed for the Japanese civilians. Then, they put their emotion aside and gathered their courage. They got to work, following orders as they had sworn to do.

Holopainen and the other airmen boarded trucks and rode over to their planes. They carried their gear – flight checklists, parachutes, helmets and flak jackets. They also carried snacks and cigarettes that Red Cross volunteers had handed out. They inspected the planes with their ground crews, who wished them well. The airmen then climbed aboard their aircraft, controlling their nerves as they went through their flight checklists in preparation for takeoff. They took their places in the long line of roaring B-29s that stretched out along the taxiway. Each B-29 would take off about a minute apart, so takeoffs were to be perfectly accomplished.

The B-29s taking off from Guam would meet up with B-29s from two other bases and with P-51 Mustang escorts, based out of Iwo Jima, whose job was to shoot down any enemy planes that tried to take down the B-29s. Holopainen's job was the next line of defense – to shoot down or scare away any enemy planes that approached his B-29. It was a big first day at work for a kid just a year out of high school – his first job. He was to help prevent a 100,000-thousand-pound heavy bomber from getting shot out of the sky by enemy Japanese. He would be flying so low that someone could shoot him from the ground. Also, his co-workers all seemed to think that most of them were going to get shot down and be captured or killed.

Holopainen was to be alone with his thoughts throughout the mission. He would sit by himself in his compartment in the tail of the plane, facing out the back window in a very exposed position. He carried aboard belts of .50 caliber bullets for his mounted twin machine guns. He climbed into his little capsule and loaded his bullets into the ammunition containers in the back of his compartment. As they got into line for takeoff, Holopainen was scared. He was most afraid of being captured. That's what so much of his training had stressed – how not to get shot down. His superiors and his buddies had told him that the Japanese were ruthless in torturing prisoners and that they beheaded a lot of the men they captured.

Holopainen's plane blasted out of Guam and headed for Tokyo. With any luck, he would sit in his compartment for the next fifteen hours, firing his machine guns when he saw enemy fire, and arrive back at his base in Guam the next day. His seat faced backwards, so he could not see Tokyo as they approached it. He could hear the fighting from far away though. The sounds of bombing grew louder and louder and then Holopainen was in battle. As his plane passed over the city, he could see Tokyo ablaze. Fires burned out of control. Japanese searchlights lit up the B-29s, and the air was filled with pieces of flak, any one of which could take down a plane. Planes, bombs and flak filled the sky. It seemed miraculous that anyone could survive this, but most did, and all went well for Holopainen. His plane flew low and fast into Tokyo, dropped its bombs on its target and roared out again through the smoke that covered the city.

LeMay's reputation as a brilliant strategist had been proven again – the mission had succeeded beyond even his own expectations. The targets had been hit, and only fourteen B-29s were lost. While that was a small percentage of loss for a B-29 mission, it was 154 sons, brothers and husbands. When Holopainen returned to his Quonset hut that night, there were five empty beds.

Holopainen went on to fly thirty-four more missions as a part of LeMay's firebombing campaign. Around the time that he had arrived in Guam, the

U.S. Marines had taken the island of Iwo Jima from Japan in a legendary battle. The U.S. had a base, therefore, on Iwo Jima. To Holopainen and the other airmen, the base on Iwo Jima was a true blessing. Iwo Jima is very close to Japan, so U.S. planes could stop there to refuel after a mission. More importantly, planes that had been severely damaged and could not make it back to Guam – and many, many were – could stop at Iwo Jima. Some planes were so badly damaged that they could not even land on Iwo Jima. Instead, their crews ditched into the ocean and waited to be rescued.

Holopainen and his fellow crewmembers flew two or three times a week, and with each mission they took the risk of being shot down or falling from the sky because of an accident or bad weather. Many friends were lost. He and his crew made it through though.

Sergeant Holopainen's story concludes in Chapter 24.

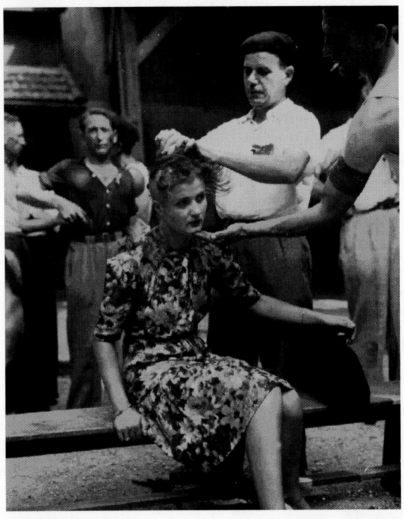

As the war ended and the Allies freed Europe from Nazi occupation, local citizens who were deemed to have conspired with or had personal relationships with the Nazis were punished by other citizens. In this photo, French citizens shave a young woman's head to punish her for having had personal relationships with Germans during the German occupation of France. Photograph dated August 29, 1944, by Photographer Smith.
Photo courtesy of the U.S. National Archives, number 111-SC-193785.

18

The Mighty 8ᵗʰ Air Force, the Last Days of the War in Europe, and the Service of First Lieutenant Paul Lahr, U.S. Army Air Forces

Paul Lahr, age 20, woke up at 3 a.m. on April 25, 1945, on an airbase in England, a long way from his home in the New York countryside. He got ready for his job that day – navigating his B-17 heavy bomber, a strongly armored, propeller-driven aircraft known as the "Flying Fortress," in the 8ᵗʰ Air Force's last full-scale air mission in Europe. By this point in the war, Germany was largely defeated and its air force, the *Luftwaffe*, lay in tatters, but it did still control an enormous armaments plant, the Skoda Arms Works, located in German-occupied Pilsen, Czechoslovakia. Skoda Arms was the chief source of armaments for the Nazi Party during the war and is estimated to have produced almost as much weaponry as that of all of Britain's armament factories combined. Russia, soon to be the archenemy of the U.S. in the Cold War, was advancing through the area and was set to take Skoda Arms. Lahr's mission was to help destroy the factory.

Lahr assembled at 5:00 a.m. with 589 heavy bombers, B-17s and B-24s, and 486 P-51 Mustang fighter escorts. They were to hit Skoda Arms and certain airfield and rail targets in southeast Germany and Czechoslovakia and then return to England, about eleven hours in the air there and back. The mission would turn out to be successful, with more than seventy percent of Skoda Arms destroyed, but the Germans had advance warning of the bombing. Much of what remained of Germany's fighting forces lay in wait for the 8ᵗʰ Air Force on April 25. The Germans would shoot down six U.S. bombers and one fighter that day, and one of those was Lahr's plane. He and his fellow crewmembers bailed out of their B-17 onto the frontlines of battle. After being rescued by U.S. airmen who had witnessed the downing, Lahr made his way back to his base in England just as World War II ended and continued to serve in Europe after the war as the Cold War was getting underway.

Only three years before getting shot down, Lahr had lived at home, one of ten children in a rural house on a dirt road outside of Geneva, New York. His father died when he was just a boy. His mother kept the family together, and four of her children served in the military. The family did not have electricity until Lahr was ten years old, and they never did get running water or indoor plumbing. People told stories of guys who never had shoes until they were drafted. Lahr never had indoor plumbing until he was drafted. Lahr joined the Army just after high school, leaving his low-tech home to serve in a high tech job in the skies over Germany.

Matching the right person to the job was key to the U.S. military's success in the war. Millions of people had to be trained for the war effort – and quickly. Inductees were given a battery of tests to determine where their talents lay and what work they should therefore do. Lahr was drafted into the Army's 75th Infantry Division and completed basic and advanced infantry training, but then he decided he didn't want to walk with the infantry. He had heard that he could sit for intelligence tests and hope to qualify for some other kind of work. He was tested and qualified for the Army Specialized Training Program, the purpose of which was to make sure there would still be college graduates if the war was long. The program, held on college campuses, combined military training together with college course work. Lahr also qualified for the Army Air Forces Cadet Program, and he opted for that.

In January of 1942, the Army Air Forces eliminated the requirement that aviation cadets have completed at least two years of college. Instead, potential cadets were tested in a variety of areas including intelligence, judgment, mental alertness, current events (interestingly, this was an important indicator of success in the cadet program), math and mechanical aptitude. They were interviewed by psychologists and also underwent testing of hand-eye coordination, reflexes, ability to perform under pressure, and vision. Cadets with lower test scores were sent to serve elsewhere in the Army.

Higher math scores were a good predictor of success in navigation training, and Lahr had scored well in math. Most cadets wanted to become pilots, but Lahr chose to be a navigator.

Lahr completed the cadet program and was commissioned into the Army Air Forces as an Aerial Navigator, 2nd Lieutenant, on November 18, 1944, at the age of nineteen. A couple of weeks later he was sent to the Rapid City Army Air Base just outside Rapid City, South Dakota. He trained for three months in Rapid City and then was sent to England, where he joined the 8th Air Force in late February of 1945.

Based out of a former school in High Wycombe, England, the 8th and 15th Air Forces, along with Britain's Royal Air Force (the RAF), executed the strategic bombing campaign of German-occupied Europe. Strategic bombing was in its infancy, and the Mighty 8th Air Force suffered many casualties as techniques for flying their missions were developed and improved. Over half of the Army Air Forces' casualties in the war were members of the Mighty 8th.

Strategic bombing was controversial for many reasons. If the bombers flew too low, they were more likely to hit their targets but also were more likely to get shot down. If bombers flew too high, the crewmen were more likely to survive their missions, but the bombers more often missed their targets. This resulted in more civilian deaths and could be considered by the enemy to be "terror bombing," bombing aimed at civilians, meant to terrorize and demoralize the civilian population. U.S. policy in Europe was against terror bombing.

Lahr's plane, the four-engine B-17 built by The Boeing Company, was known as the "Flying Fortress" because it was heavily armored and had enormous firepower. When it was first developed, experts believed it could fly unescorted, as it was better equipped than any other aircraft to take huge barrages of enemy fire and still make it back to base after a mission. The Mighty 8th suffered many casualties, however, early in the war, flying unescorted missions. Later, Mustang fighter planes, designed and built by North American Aviation, originally for England's Royal Air Force, were employed as escorts for the bombers. While the heavy bombers such as Lahr's had a crew of several men, the Mustang fighters were one-man planes whose pilots fired enormous, mounted machine guns at the enemy to protect the bombers. At its height, the Mighty 8th could deploy more than 2,000 bombers and 1,000 fighters on a single mission.

Lahr's fifth and last mission was to bomb the Skoda Arms Works. Amazingly, Germany knew about the mission. About one hour after the bombers and fighters had stormed out of England, Eisenhower announced over the British radio station BBC that bombers were heading to Czechoslovakia and that, consequently, workers at Skoda Arms might be in harm's way. This announcement surely saved many civilian lives – out of the approximately 40,000 people who worked at the plant, only six were killed and four injured – but it meant that the Germans were aware of the mission and had hours to prepare.

It was a beautiful day with no clouds over Germany, but a little cloud cover hung over the factory, so the 400 bombers turned around in a big, 360-degree turn to see if the clouds would clear. It takes a while for 400 heavy bombers to turn around, and the Germans were ready. They had the Mighty 8th in their sights and opened fire.

The Germans were firing 88 mm anti-aircraft shells. The 8th Fighter Command of P-51s was trying its best to protect the heavy bombers. The bombers could defend themselves as well and were shooting and throwing out their chaff – little pieces of tinfoil – to mess up the Germans' radar. Looking down, Lahr could see the Germans firing at the chafe. Then, Lahr's plane was hit.

Lahr's plane got shot and lost an engine. That made them lose altitude and speed, and they couldn't keep up with the others in their group. The Germans were attacking stragglers like Lahr, but his plane escaped that and made it back another hour and got pretty far into Germany, near Munich. Their plane was in bad shape, though. Near Munich, they lost another engine – it was overloaded – and this caused them to descend to about 10,000 feet. Then, the number-two engine caught on fire, and flames burst throughout the plane, all the way to the tail. Lahr and his crewmates prepared their parachutes, and they all bailed out of their plane, floating down through the sky onto enemy land.

At this point, Lahr had seen a lot of trouble – he had just parachuted out of a burning plane after being shot at, losing two engines and plunging ten thousand feet. Now his luck had turned. He and his crewmates all survived the bailout, and they avoided capture by the German military or – worse – by angry mobs of German civilians.

The people of Germany had suffered grievously by this point in the war, having endured years of bombings by Allied forces and brutal treatment by Russian occupiers. Many Germans had lost everything in the war. Also, only two months before, in February 1945, U.S. and British bombers had destroyed Germany's most beautiful and historic city, Dresden. In massive fires caused by the bombings, tens of thousands of civilians were killed, the exact number of which is still debated today.

The German people naturally felt vengeful toward Americans, and Lahr and the others had been advised to stay away from German civilians. They had been told that if they landed in Germany, try to surrender to the German Air Force or Army. Lahr found it interesting that surrender was discussed at all. Merely three or four months before he was shot down, they were still being told that it was their duty under military law not to surrender but to avoid capture and try to resist and escape. At this point, the Allies were set to win, so surrendering would not affect the outcome of the war but could save some lives of the boys who got shot down.

Lahr and his nine crewmates all landed safely, scattered over several miles. He landed near his aerial engineer, and they hid in the woods together. They didn't know if they were in Allied or German territory because the front lines were moving hourly. After several minutes they heard a jeep and American voices – they were rescued! It turned out that Americans had seen the bail out. Some of the legendary 101st Airborne troops were going to chow when they saw Lahr's plane flying over. They saw the smoke and the bailout and immediately sent jeeps out to find them. Then they took the crew back to a castle where they were staying.

Lahr's B-17 was one of seven planes that the Germans shot down that day. He and his crewmates all survived, but others were not so fortunate. Two airmen were captured by Nazis and turned over to Allied forces. It was reported that several survivors were taken prisoner and then killed by Nazis. Forty-two men were reported missing in action that day, and the fate of many remains a mystery.

Stranded in Germany, Lahr and his fellow crewmates had to figure out how to get back to their base in England. They had a crazy trip, hitching back to England, bumming rides with rear guard people running supplies. They stayed in a resort town for a few days, then got a ride to Paris, and then they bummed a ride on a plane to England, and four or five days later, the war ended, about three months sooner than Lahr and his crewmates had predicted.

Lieutenant Lahr's story concludes in Chapter 24.

National Archives photograph of healthy-looking German POWs being paid for their work in a POW prison in Michigan. Prisoners in camps across the U.S. were paid for their work and enjoyed good food, sports and movies. They pursued hobbies such as gardening, music and painting. Some people believed the prisoners were coddled.

19

Dunn's Story Continues: Surviving German Prison Camps

After POW processing in Frankfurt, Staff Sergeant Dunn was handcuffed and put on a railroad boxcar where he rode with other prisoners for two days with no food and no plumbing. Dunn was sent to *Stalag-Luft* (Air Prison) *VI* in Lithuania, which was a prison that had been around since the start of the war. While conditions at this prison were more humane than the prisons Dunn would later endure, it was still abysmal. Dunn kept a journal and wrote about this first prison, "If I mention food and toilet facilities often, it is because they were so inadequate and so humbling."

The prisoners had set up some games to pass the time and had put together a radio that they hid from the guards. They listened to news of the war from the British radio station BBC and wrote down the news on a piece of paper so they could share it with the others. "Someone was stationed at the door while the news was being read. If a German guard appeared, someone had to eat the paper the news was written on. It tasted awful. But news from England's BBC was a link with our yesteryears," Dunn wrote.

The prisoners received food packages from the International Red Cross every so often and ate whatever was left after the guards looted them. The Germans fed the men very little, mainly a brown bread "not fit for a farm animal to eat," said Dunn. After about three months, the men were skeletal, according to photographs Dunn kept. "We laid around all day and grew skinny," Dunn wrote. The first thing the men thought about when they awoke in the mornings was food, and food was a central topic of conversation. Talking about getting shot down was not always welcome. Every prisoner had his story about getting shot down, and many of the men grew tired of listening to them.

At night the prisoners were locked in their rooms, about fifty men to a room that should have accommodated twenty-five, and they shared a thirty-gallon bucket in the room as their toilet. The single window in Dunn's room was covered so the room was pitch black and the men bumped into each other at night.

One evening, the guards neglected to lock a door, and the next morning a prisoner left his room a few minutes early. Dunn heard a gunshot and saw the man lying dead outside. He was a U.S. prisoner named Walter whose plane had been shot down on January 24, a month before Dunn was shot down. Walter had been a tail gunner with the 96th squadron, and at the time he was killed he was sick with dysentery, an intestinal infection that many of the prisoners suffered from. After he died, his body just lay there for several days, until the guards allowed the prisoners to bury their friend. Dunn witnessed other prisoners being shot to death when they tried to escape.

The Germans were losing the war in large part due to a lack of resources and could not afford to feed and guard prisoners. Releasing the prisoners, however, was not an option because, among other reasons, the Germans wanted to use them as a bargaining chip in negotiations at the end of the war. To keep this bit of leverage, though, the Germans had to make sure that the Allies could not rescue the prisoners. Consequently, as the front lines of the war moved into Germany, the Germans moved the prisoners closer into the areas that they still held onto.

Dunn was imprisoned at *Stalag-Luft VI* from March 5, 1944, until July of 1944. On April 28, 1944, Dunn's parents received a Western Union telegram informing them that their son "IS A PRISONER OF WAR OF THE GERMAN GOVERNMENT." When Dunn's brother Bill saw the telegram, he enlisted in the service with the thought of going to save him. After he enlisted, Bill was assigned to serve in the Navy. He was stationed in Europe, but he never had any opportunity to save his brother.

On July 14, 1944, the prisoners in *Stalag-Luft VI* who were well enough to walk were moved to *Stalag-Luft IV*, traveling under horrific conditions, in one of what became known as the "Forced Marches" of POWs in Germany. First, the two thousand men were handcuffed and piled into a small boat in which they traveled for two days with no toilets, no ventilation and no food other than whatever they may have brought with them. After the prisoners disembarked in Swinemunde, Germany, guards forced the weak, starved men to march at double time for two miles, to their next prison, brutalizing them each step of the way. The guards pushed the lines of men forward by attacking them with guns, bayonets and dogs. Men were horribly injured, and if they had managed to hang onto any personal items to this point, most of those were dropped as they struggled to stay upright.

Stalag-Luft IV was miserable from the start. "When we arrived, bayonetted, bitten and gun-butted we ran into more misery. Lined up outside the camp were many large German soldiers. As we entered the camp, they took a great delight in slugging every POW they could get their hands on. We could not fight back. Death would follow," Dunn wrote.

By January of 1945, the Nazis were on the run, and that month Dunn and his fellow prisoners from *Stalag-Luft IV* were put on trains and sent to *Stalag-Luft III*, in Nuremburg, now part of Poland. They rode in boxcars called "forty or eights" because they could hold forty men or eight horses. The prisoners rode eighty men to a car for seven days with no plumbing. As they rode in the boxcars, they could not see outside, but they could hear a lot of bombing, sirens and other activity and could tell from this that the Allies were taking Germany and that their ordeal would be over soon. Yet despite all that Dunn and his fellow prisoners had suffered, the next prison would be the worst yet.

During their stay at *Stalag-Luft III*, the men suffered from fleas that "chewed on us all day long," according to Dunn. The men had lice, and bugs crawled everywhere. "At meal time we had watered-down soup containing bugs. We tried to count them as they appeared. Eventually we ate them. Not too tasty, but we kept alive," Dunn wrote. Having reached this Nuremburg camp, the prisoners were at their limits of survival. "By this time we had become so weak, we mostly lay in our beds. We slept four to a bed, which was against Army regulations. How appreciative we would have been to fulfill dreams of fresh new clothing, steak with baked potatoes and a comfortable bed. But it was survival that was uppermost in our minds," Dunn wrote.

Stalag-Luft III had been built to house captured pilots, mainly from the British Royal Air Force (the RAF), and these pilots were very focused on escaping. By some accounts, more escape attempts were made from here than from any other German prison camp. Hundreds of escape tunnels were built, though most were discovered before they could be used, and some of the most famous escapes of the war were from *Stalag-Luft III*.

One famous escape was led by RAF Major Roger Bushel, who led prisoners in the excavation of an enormous tunnel – over 300 feet long. In March of 1944, more than seventy RAF officers escaped the prison. Hitler launched a massive search for the escapees and ordered that they be executed. The German Gestapo and the Criminal Police Force shot and killed fifty of the men who had escaped, including Bushel.

After a few months in *Stalag-Luft III*, the prisoners had to move again. By this point, the Germans could not spare any transportation, so the prisoners had to endure a Forced March of ninety miles. "We could hardly stand let alone walk," Dunn wrote. They walked four hours at a time, took one-hour breaks and slept in barns or outside in fields, sometimes in the rain. The war was almost over, and some men reported that U.S. planes flew over them in solidarity as they marched.

After a week of marching, the men arrived at *Stalag VII-A* on April 12, 1945. At this prison, Dunn was put in a large barn. The toilet was a hole in the ground with a pole over it. "Careful boys and keep your balance to prevent a miserable fall into that cavity," Dunn wrote. At this point more than 130,000 prisoners were held at *Stalag VII-A*, which was also known as "Mooseburg," the name of the nearby town. The emaciated men in the barn with Dunn were too weak to move. They lay on hay on the floor, around the clock, for almost a month, until U.S. soldiers rescued them. Dunn, who points out that they were liberated on April 29, before the war ended, wrote about that day in his journal.

> *[W]e could hear guns in the distance. The German guards were running for their lives. We knew that our friends were coming. It was General Patton's Tank Division. At 1:30 p.m. the American flag was raised over the camp. We had been liberated.*

Soldiers from the 14th Armored Division of Patton's 3rd Army had arrived, and Patton visited the camp himself. Next was the major task of transporting more than 130,000 former prisoners, many of them weak and ill, out of the prison. Many of them were too emaciated to stand, speak or even acknowledge that they were being rescued. The soldiers who rescued them were heartbroken and furious. The U.S. had treated German prisoners extremely well.

On May 10, Dunn was taken by truck to Reims, France. Dunn and about 2,000 others in his group enjoyed getting hosed down with de-lousing medication, taking warm showers, being clean for the first time since being imprisoned and putting on fresh clothes. Dunn, like many others, had never fully bathed and had never changed his clothes throughout the fourteen months he had been kept prisoner.

By this point, Dunn had reached his physical limit and was deathly ill. He was rushed to a U.S. military hospital and treated for jaundice and then for hepatitis. He was hospitalized for more than a month and, all his dreams of good food notwithstanding, was too sick to eat. At one point, the only available bed for Dunn was in the psychiatric ward, for men who had broken down mentally during the war. One of Dunn's friends in that ward – "we were all friends," Dunn wrote of his fellow prisoners – rode an imaginary bicycle all day and another crushed light bulbs and ate them.

Sergeant Dunn's story concludes in Chapter 24.

The Liberation of the Concentration Camps

During the final months of the war in Europe, as the U.S. and other Allied forces fought their way across German-occupied Poland and into the German homeland, they began to discover the hellish Nazi concentration camps. The 4ᵗʰ Armoured Division was the first to discover the camps. They were stunned by what they saw. They could never have imagined that humans could be so badly abused. They didn't know that humans could be thoroughly evil. At the camps, the soldiers saw thousands of starved, brutalized, diseased and emaciated people, most of them dying. They looked like living skeletons. They didn't look much different than the dead, which were stacked in piles, dumped into trucks and buried in stacks in the ground. The camps were nightmarish.

In April of 1945, Allied Supreme Commander General Dwight D. Eisenhower wrote that he had personally visited a camp near Gotha, Germany, the first camp to be liberated by the Allies, in order to bear witness in case anyone ever tried to deny the Nazi atrocities. Eisenhower was a wise and prescient man.

Eisenhower requested that the military fly leaders of the U.S. Congress and prominent members of the press to Europe to view the atrocities at the camps. He wanted as many witnesses as possible. He ordered soldiers to bear witness as well. These hardened soldiers had been through war; they had heard people scream out in agony; they had seen people get burned, disfigured and die, but what the soldiers saw at the concentration camps, what the Nazis had done to the Jewish people and the other prisoners at these camps, was beyond anything they had seen in their worst nightmares. This was the manifestation of evil.

General Patton, the great, brave leader of men into battle, accompanied Eisenhower to the camp near Gotha. The camp was known as Ohrdruf and was a sub-camp of the Buchenwald camp. Patton could not bear to go in.

The Allies worked diligently to save the survivors. The camps had been run on a massive scale, and it was a massive undertaking to get medical treatment to the former prisoners and get them on their feet. Most of the Jewish prisoners from Poland and Germany did not want to return to their home countries. They wanted to be sent to Palestine.

An American soldier guarding German prisoners, circa 1944. Photo courtesy of the U.S. National Archives, number 208-YE-105.

20

Santoro's Story Continues: The End of the War in Europe

After "drafting" Salvatore Santoro, the Army shipped him off to France, to a base just outside the Bay of Biscay, where the six-year-long Battle of the Atlantic was winding down. The battle was vitally important to Allied success in the war. As Churchill described it, "The Battle of the Atlantic was the dominating factor all through the war. Never for one moment could we forget that everything happening elsewhere, on land, at sea, or in the air depended ultimately on its outcome."

Strategically located off the west coast of France, just south of England, the Bay of Biscay was key to the Germans' campaign to use U-boats to attack Allied supply ships. It was an absolutely critical location for both sides in the war, and fighting there was intense. The Battle of the Atlantic had continued throughout all the years of the war and ended just when the war itself ended, about a month after Santoro arrived at his base near the Bay of Biscay. Hitler had sent a couple of his best divisions there to fight, and the Allies had been blasted pretty hard.

The War in Europe ended on May 7, 1945, when Gen. Alfred Jodl, Chief of Staff of the German Army, signed four identical surrender documents to the U.S., Britain, France and Russia, at Allied headquarters in Reims, France. German officials then commanded their troops to cease all hostilities and surrender to the Allied forces they had just been fighting.

After years of battle and years of watching their friends get killed and their homeland get destroyed, however, not all German soldiers were ready to follow the order to walk over to the troops they had been fighting, hand over their guns and be taken into custody. Some refused to obey the command to surrender and became "werewolves," shooting any Germans they saw who were attempting to surrender. Werewolves also reportedly shot Americans who were accepting surrenders or who were guarding camps of surrendered German troops. Santoro's new buddies at his base had taught him a bit about the lay of the land, so he knew about the werewolves. It was the scariest day of his life when his unit trapped two German units at the Bay of Biscay and forced them to surrender, with the war barely ended.

A few weeks later, heading to a new post in Germany on a cold, dismal, rainy day, Santoro almost died in a battalion of troop transport trucks. The trucks, known as "6 x 6's," were equipped with benches for the troops along the sides and space in the middle for the men's duffle bags. The trucks were covered with canvas tops and looked liked old, covered wagons. There was no place left to sit on a bench in his truck, so Santoro climbed onto the tall pile of duffle bags in the middle and fell asleep. About an hour and a half into the ride, halfway to their destination, their convoy of 6 x 6's stopped for a Red Cross truck that was serving coffee and donuts. Santoro woke up from napping, got off the truck and collapsed on the ground, unable to move.

"He must be a [   ] drunk," someone said, though Santoro never drank. As it happened, the covers on the trucks were trapping the carbon monoxide from the engine inside, and he – lying high atop the duffels where the gas had risen – was poisoned. The commander radioed medics, who said, "There's nothing we can do for that, so just see if he lives or not." The Red Cross people had some ammonia vials and revived him. If Santoro had stayed on that truck and skipped the treat, he never would have awakened from his nap. The convoy continued on in the rain with the tarps removed. Coffee and donuts – which he had longed to buy during the Depression – had saved his life.

By the end of the war, Germany and its people, like most of Europe, had been crushed. Cities lay in bombed-out rubble, and entire streets, business- es, schools and hospitals were gone. Starving, homeless people searched for food, shelter and safety. During the war, Russian soldiers had raped the girls and women of Germany on a horrifically massive scale, a practice condoned by Stalin, and the Allies had dropped tons of bombs on the German home- land, leaving mass destruction. The German population's hatred toward their enemies had naturally built up over the years and was not to be eliminated with the signing of peace treaties. Some Allied commanders told troops that if they were in danger of being captured, they were safer being taken by the German military than by German civilians.

Santoro came to realize just how vehemently the German civilians hated the Americans. One evening after the war had ended, five of Santoro's young Army buddies went to a German bar to enjoy some beer, while Santoro, who was older, stayed at the post because he didn't like to drink. His friends came home sick. The Germans had put poison in their drinks. The boys were terribly sick all night long. By morning, they all were dead.

The war in Europe was officially over, but the continent and its people would continue to suffer from their wounds for a very long time.

Private First Class Santoro's story concludes in Chapter 24.

21

Cooke's Story Continues: Rebuilding the Philippines at the End of the War in the Pacific

Towards the end of 1944, Sergeant Cooke's assignment at P.O. Box 1142 ended, and the Army had him train for a completely different job – as a technician. "This is so typical of being in the Army. You never know what you're going to get into," Cooke wrote home.

Cooke was sent first to Camp Claiborne in Louisiana, where he could not get used to the heat, humidity or the razorback hogs that ran wild there. He also trained at a depot in Illinois where he encountered some of the nicest people he had ever met. When Cooke got leave for a few hours, he and his buddies would walk around town, go to the movies or hang around at the USO club drinking coffee and talking to local people who would come in to meet the boys and keep them company. Cooke couldn't believe how generous the local people were. He was very touched on several occasions when, as he and his friends were leaving their base, they were met at the gate by locals who would drive them home, share dinner with them, and drive them back to the base. Cooke realized that people had small rations of gas and was very appreciative of their kindness.

After training with engineers – "I have no idea of why I am training with engineers," he wrote home – he was sent to California and issued a rifle. It was January of 1945, and all he knew was that he was going to the Pacific. It turned out that he was headed for Manila, the capital of the Philippines, and would arrive there just as battle was winding down.

The fight for Manila had been ferocious. The Japanese had started suicide missions in the Philippines at the end of 1944. They were getting desperate. General MacArthur would not lose the Philippines this time, after the Japanese had made him retreat from there at the beginning of the war. MacArthur's forces landed on the island in late 1944 and fought their way to Manila. By the end of March, the U.S. had beaten the Japanese to the point where they no longer ruled the government, but many Japanese soldiers remained there and continued to fight. They hid in the jungle and attacked Americans with sniper fire.

Cooke arrived in Manila aboard a transport ship named the *USNS Blatchford (T-AP-153)*, a ship that would go on to serve in the Korean and Vietnam wars. It was April 12, 1945, the night that President Roosevelt died. The War in Europe was ending and the War in the Pacific would end in a few months.

Cooke climbed off the *Blatchford* onto a landing ship, with no escort, worrying about Kamikazes. There was no doubt he was in a combat zone. When he got to shore, he could hear gunshots. He noticed that part of the road had been taped off and was told that it was the part that was safe to drive on – it had been tested for land mines. Cooke and his new Pacific-theater buddies rode aboard trucks into Manila. They could see dead Japanese hanging in elevator shafts. The sounds of gunfire were all around.

Cooke's mission was to help rebuild the city. He lived in a bombed-out building with no windows, which was typical lodging on the island. Virtually every structure in the Philippines had been damaged or destroyed during the war. Cooke was assigned to run the headquarters' switchboard, having been trained in electrical engineering. He set up outlying areas with communications systems and then hired and trained Filipinos to operate the entire system.

Cooke ran into sniper fire once, several months into his mission while accompanying a courier to Clark Airfield. The road was a straight shot through a bunch of rice paddies, but they had to zigzag around dead Japanese lying on the road. On the way home, in the dark, the two men heard a loud "bang" – one of their tires had blown. Cooke held a light while the courier changed the flat. All of a sudden they heard 'snap, snap.' It was gunfire.

The courier told Cooke to douse the light and protect him while he changed the tire. Cooke grabbed a Thompson machine gun, lowered it, and walked around the jeep firing tracer bullets into the rice paddies. It took awhile, but after a couple turns around the jeep, Cooke noticed that the sniper fire had stopped. His buddy finished changing the tire, and they continued on home, still dodging the dead bodies on the road.

Once the fighting had stopped, Cooke's work was somewhat like a regular job, though in a bombed out, tropical locale. When his workday ended, he would relax with friends, Filipino and American, boys and girls. They drove around in the jeep he was allowed to use, going to tiki bars and having parties on the beach.

Sergeant Cooke's story concludes in Chapter 24.

General Curtis Emerson LeMay.
Photo courtesy of the U.S. Air Force.

22

Fire Bombing, Japan's Surrender and the Service of Captain Reed Bertolette, U.S. Army Air Forces

While the war in Europe ended in early May of 1945, General LeMay's 20th Air Force was still continuing its bombing missions over Japan, trying to force Japan into submission and surrender. Reed ("Chick") Bertolette served in the 20th Air Force, working as an engineer aboard a B-29 Superfortress in twenty-eight of LeMay's bombing missions over Japan. He was in the air the day after the 20th dropped the first atomic bomb. After Japan finally surrendered at the end of the summer, Bertolette stayed on a while to help carry out humanitarian missions.

Before the U.S entered the war, Bertolette had been studying hard and enjoying himself at college. When Bertolette arrived there in the fall of 1940, Yale University, located in New Haven, Connecticut, was home to Ivy League privilege, top-notch academics and spirited fun at weekend football games. This would all change. Yale has a long history of military tradition and pride, and these traits were revived whole-heartedly on campus when Japan attacked the U.S. at Pearl Harbor in December of 1941. It seemed to Bertolette that the military had all but taken over Yale. Like many of his classmates, Bertolette joined the service while he was still a student. He became a cadet in the Army Air Forces Technical Training Command (the AAFTTC), which operated a program at Yale.

After the U.S. entered the war, Yale basically became a military base. Like many colleges and universities throughout the country, Yale contracted with the government to provide resources for the war effort. The university rented out six of its eight residential colleges, which are similar to dormitories, to the Army and Navy. More than 20,000 service members received training at Yale. Bertolette felt that at Yale the attitude was "let's do all we can to get the enemy." Though a member of the class of 1944, he graduated in 1943 because of the war. Yale sped things up for the young men, so they could graduate early and get off to war. They took courses over the summer, and the school gave them a semester of credit for their cadet work.

The AAFTTC had taken over Yale's Old Campus, a large complex of academic buildings, dormitories and a four-acre green. Bertolette listened to Glenn Miller's Army Air Forces Band playing in the mornings in the Yale Commons, a huge dining hall on the Old Campus where students gathered. Bertolette could hear them playing jazz while he and his group were doing their maneuvers, but then the band would switch to military music as the cadets marched by. Sometimes the marches were jazzy too, as Miller was keen on adding swing rhythms to military marches – he wanted to modernize military music. Once Miller was questioned about this and reportedly told a Yale camp commander that he wasn't playing the same marches from the last war and hoped they weren't flying the same planes either.

In addition to the cadet training, Bertolette studied business administration and industrial engineering. Combining cadet training with college courses was hard work for the cadets. Bertolette graduated from Yale in December of 1943 in a pared-down, wartime graduation ceremony and finished the cadet course as a second lieutenant. He went on for more training at a country club in Boca Raton, Florida – it seemed as if the whole country had been taken over by the war effort. They had very fancy digs, but they slept eight guys in a room in bunk beds. The golf course was turned into an obstacle course.

After Florida, Bertolette trained on the B-29 Superfortress at Pratt Air Force Base in Kansas, observed a B-29 being built at the Boeing Company in Seattle, Washington, received operational instruction at Lowry Airfield, in Denver, Colorado, and was then ready for war. He would be based in Guam working as an engineer aboard a B-29 called *City of Modesto*, named after the pilot's hometown.

Air power itself was still relatively new in warfare, and many military experts thought it should be used only as an auxiliary to ground and naval forces -- providing cover to the Army in battles and to the Navy at sea, conducting aerial photography for mission planning, and transporting troops and supplies. Most trained airmen, however, believed that air power should also be employed in warfare as an independent fighting force – the air force. Under this theory, the U.S. Army Air Forces was established in 1941 and co-existed with the U.S. Army Air Corps until the war ended. After the war, the Air Force was established as an independent branch of the military.

Central to the idea of the air force as an independent fighting force was the concept of "strategic bombing," whereby bombs would be dropped in key locations over enemy territory, destroying the enemy's transportation centers, armaments factories and other means of carrying out war. Strategists would map out the key elements of the enemy's infrastructure and develop intricate plans to eliminate them until the enemy could no longer fight. Planning what to strike and striking with precision are the key elements of strategic bombing.

The leader of the Army Air Forces during the war was Four-Star General Henry ("Hap") Arnold, who had been taught to fly by the Wright brothers and who was awarded a permanent fifth star after he retired from the service after the war. Arnold was dedicated to the development of an independent air force and to the use of strategic bombing. Unfortunately, as the war entered its last months, it was apparent that the strategic bombing campaigns in Europe had been less than ideal. One reason for this was that Allied ground commanders were able to pre-empt the bombing plans so that they could use the aircraft to support their ground operations.

When the U.S. began strategic bombing in Japan in late 1944, Arnold wanted to make sure that air strategies could not be interrupted or undermined by ground or naval forces. Arnold established the 20th Air Force to carry out the strategic bombing of Japan and was able to persuade the White House that the 20th should report to him, not to the Pacific Theater commanders, General MacArthur and Admiral Nimitz.

The 20th began its strategic bombing of Japan in late November of 1944, using the new B-29 Superfortress. The 21st Bomber Command, which was based in the Marianas Islands, where Guam is located, carried out the extremely challenging campaign. Arnold put General Haywood Hansel in charge. Hansel's job was to take inexperienced crews, put them into untested aircraft and have them strategically bomb Japan, which had challenging wind currents, territory uncharted by the U.S. and was a thousand miles away from the U.S. bases in the Marianas. When Hansel was unable to overcome all of these obstacles, Arnold fired him, just a couple of months into the campaign.

Arnold brought in General Curtis LeMay to replace Hansel. LeMay had to figure out how to use the B-29s to destroy Japan's ability to wage war. His unofficial deadline was the autumn of 1945. If Japan was still at war by that time, the Allies planned to invade under a plan called Operation Downfall. More than 700,000 Allied troops would land in Japan, on November 1, 1945, and fight to the death. Japan was expecting an invasion and was training troops and civilians – even children and the elderly –to protect their home-land to the point of suicide. The U.S. expected the battle to be a bloodbath.

LeMay had tremendous organizational talents and carefully implemented his ideas for change. He had the B-29 crews train until they worked precisely together as perfect teams and then made sure they stayed together as teams. He put the best crews at the head of flight formations and inexperienced crews at the back until they had proven themselves. He standardized flight checklists and streamlined maintenance procedures. Most importantly, in one of the most controversial strategies in military history, Lemay employed the use of incendiary or firebombing on a massive scale.

In strategic bombing, civilians may be killed when bombs miss their tar-gets, when targets are close to human populations or when bombs cause fires. In firebombing, entire swaths of land are leveled, and thousands upon thou-sands of people are killed in vast fires. LeMay, a larger than life figure who always kept a cigar clenched between his jaws, had a legendary reputation for bravery, and he was a fierce warrior. He was unapologetic about the use of mass incendiary bombing, believing that this strategy would end the war sooner, with fewer lives lost in the end.

Bertolette arrived at Harmon Field, the AAF base in Guam, in late February of 1945, about a month into LeMay's tenure. Bertolette flew in twenty-eight missions from Guam to Japan in his B-29. The flight time in a mission was about fifteen hours – about seven hours to Japan and then back to Guam, all the while trying not to get shot down, run out of gas or experi-ence an operational problem and drop from the sky. The 20th Air Force lost more than 500 B-29s in its campaign against the Japanese homeland. The crews were well aware how risky their missions were.

The crews would return from a mission, rest up for a few days, and then go on another mission. Guam was almost unimaginably hot, humid and boring. Hanging around on the beach, playing cards and other games and going swimming kept the crews occupied when they were on the ground. The Army supplied the men with sports equipment, little paperback books, which were a novelty, and screened movies for the men to watch. Writing letters to the folks back at home and – best of all – reading letters from home were Bertolette's favorite things to do between missions.

As an engineer, Bertolette's job was to make sure the gas settings were right and that they had enough fuel to get back to Guam. By the end of a mission they were usually almost out of fuel. Fuel planning was one of the key elements in the campaign over Japan – the missions were extremely long and the planes often were delayed when they encountered the strong wind currents over Japan. Getting shot down or having to bail out of their planes over Japan was of course the biggest fear. Bertolette had been told repeatedly that the Japanese were taking prisoners and chopping their heads off.

One of the advantages of the B-29 Superfortress was that it could fly higher than its predecessor plane, the B-19 Flying Fortress, because it was pressurized. LeMay, however, had his crews fly lower. Bertolette thought at first that LeMay was nuts, that they'd be sitting ducks, but after flying a few missions at the lower altitude, he realized that they would be "okay," though not safe. There was nothing safe about these missions – but flying lower would dramatically improve bombing accuracy and advance the strategic objective.

Around the same time as the Tokyo raid, the U.S. enjoyed victory in the famous battle for Iwo Jima and established a base there. The crews were very grateful to be able to stop in Iwo Jima to refuel as they flew back and forth from Japan on their missions. The Seabees had another enormous construction project underway on Iwo Jima -- they were building a large hospital. The U.S. was preparing for a tremendous increase in U.S. casualties in Operation Downfall, scheduled for the fall of 1945.

By June, Japan's defenses were so soft that the B-29s were dropping leaflets announcing their bombing missions in advance so people could seek safety. The Japanese military was so weak it didn't matter if it knew about the U.S. raids ahead of time. Each B-29 bomber also dropped hundreds of thousands of propaganda leaflets telling the Japanese people that their military had forced their emperor – whom the Japanese worshipped as divine – into a war that Japan could never win. The U.S. was trying to sever Japanese people's blind faith in their leadership as another step toward forcing the Japanese government to surrender.

The U.S. missions had traumatized the civilian population of Japan and had cut off Japan from its supply lines, so neither the civilians nor the military could obtain food, fuel and other necessities. As the summer went on, it seemed that Japan would have to surrender at any moment. Nevertheless, in August, President Truman ordered LeMay to drop the atomic bombs. LeMay didn't think this was necessary – he thought Japan's surrender was imminent. LeMay followed orders though.

On August 6, 1945, a B-29 left its base in the Marianas and dropped an atomic bomb over the city of Hiroshima, Japan. An enormous mushroom-shaped cloud filled the sky, and radiation poisoning filled the air. More than eighty percent of the city's buildings were destroyed and more than eighty thousand people were killed instantly. Thousands more died in the following weeks from radiation poisoning. Thousands of other people suffered for years from burns and radiation poisoning.

The plane that dropped the bomb was named *The Enola Gay*, and it was piloted by Col. Paul W. Tibbets, who had named the plane after his mother. *The Enola Gay* was a part of the 313th Wing of the 21st Bomb Group – Bertolette was in the 314th Wing of that group. After the atomic bomb was dropped, Japan and the U.S. continued to wage war. B-29 missions continued in the days following the atomic bomb, and Bertolette was in the air the next day – on a mission in which one B-29 was lost – when he heard about the atomic attack.

On the day after the first atomic bomb was dropped, Soviet Russia invaded Manchuria, a declaration of war on Japan. This dragged the already heavily weakened Japanese into war on another front, against a new enemy and ended any hope on Japan's part that it could use the Soviets to help negotiate a favorable surrender to the U.S. Then, on August 9, a B-29 named *Bockscar*, piloted by Major Charles W. Sweeney, dropped the second and last atomic bomb of the war on Nagasaki, Japan, killing an estimated 25,000 to 35,000 people instantly. Thousands of more people died later from radiation poisoning.

On August 15, 1945, Japanese Emperor Hirohito ordered Japan's soldiers to stop fighting. It was the first time the Japanese public had ever heard the voice of their deified emperor. On September 2, 1945, Japanese General

Yoshijiro Umeza, Chief of the Army General Staff, formally surrendered, unconditionally, to Admiral Nimitz on September 2, 1945, in Tokyo Bay, aboard the *USS Missouri*. Operation Downfall was cancelled, and hundreds of thousands of casualties – U.S. and Japanese – were prevented.

Whether Japan surrendered due to a single cause or because of a combination of events has been debated in all the years since the war. Some people say that LeMay's firebombing campaign itself would have caused Japan to surrender and that Truman made a mistake in not realizing that. Others argue that Truman agreed that LeMay's strategy was working and called for the atomic bombs to be dropped not only to end World War II but also as a show of force in the Cold War that followed on the tails of World War II. LeMay himself was an ardent supporter of showing force as a way to avoid war, and he spearheaded the use of that strategy in the Cold War. A third view is that Truman's advisors were certain that Japan would not have surrendered before Operation Downfall if the U.S. had not dropped the atomic bombs. Under this view, Japan had known for a very long time that it could not win the war but as a matter of honor would not surrender – it would fight until it was destroyed. The choice was whether to destroy Japan with Operation Downfall or with the atomic bombs, according to this view.

More than half a million people were killed in the firebombings of Japan, and LeMay's campaign has been strongly criticized. LeMay, who died in 1990, was one of the most highly decorated military members in U.S. history. He remained committed to his belief for the rest of his life that the use of heavy force saves lives in the long run. After the war, one of LeMay's many accomplishments was to build the Strategic Air Command of the Air Force, the seat of the U.S.'s overwhelming nuclear capability during the Cold War.

LeMay's firebombing campaign and the atomic bombs have been highly criticized over the years. When the war ended, however, the people who had endured the war, military and civilian, widely celebrated LeMay as a hero.

Captain Bertolette's story concludes in Chapter 24.

23

Cancelling Operation Downfall
And the Service of Sergeant James Astor, U.S. Army

James Astor was born into a farm family in 1926, in the little town of Arlington, Iowa, about seventy miles north of Cedar Rapids. Iowa is prairie land and can brag of some of the best planting soil in the world, but during the 1920's, the bountiful farmland in Iowa became almost worthless. Encouraged to expand during World War I, U.S. farmers took on debt to invest in land and equipment. They produced huge amounts of farm goods for Europe during the war, but when the war ended, the European countries that the U.S. had been feeding began to restrict food exports from the U.S. The expanded U.S. industry was now overproducing in relation to demand for its goods. Prices for farm goods and farmers' incomes plummeted -- the U.S. farm industry had collapsed. Many farmers were caught up in a bind: their incomes had taken a nosedive; they were saddled with debt; and their land was worth a fraction of what they had paid for it. There seemed to be no way out of trouble – in many cases the price a farmer could get for his crop was less than his cost to grow it.

Astor was the fourth of ten children, and by the time he was only three years old, his parents could no longer afford to raise him. Astor's family lost their farm in 1929, and his parents could not feed him or his brother. "I was shifted out to another family," Astor explains. The toddler moved into town with foster parents, about a mile or two down the road from where his parents were living. His foster parents, immigrants from Norway, were kind to him, but he never again lived with his own family. When he turned eighteen, near the end of the war, he joined the Army. After the war, he worked hard for years to make a life for himself, his wife and his children.

As hard as life had become for Iowans during the Roaring Twenties, Iowa's economy deteriorated dramatically after the 1929 stock market crash. Former farmers like Astor's father were trying to get jobs, and factories in Iowa were struggling with labor unions and with desperate, unemployed men willing to cross picket lines and work as scabs. Farmers in Iowa, once conservative, peaceful people, were now staging protests.

Militant farmers around the state dumped milk and set up roadblocks to stop other farmers from going to market with their goods. The Iowa National Guard was called in when farmers disrupted farm foreclosure proceedings, and at one point, farmers pulled a foreclosure judge from his courtroom and threatened him with bodily harm. Not all farmers participated in the protests. Many sneaked their products into the back doors of markets. Others felt embarrassed by the protest movement: farming was regarded as very honorable work, and farmers enjoyed their reputation as respected gentlemen, businessmen and community leaders.

Astor certainly believed that farm life was superior to living in town. Growing up in a poor area was not easy. Though his foster parents were very kind to him and he did visit his parents, Astor encountered too much of the harshness of the adult world.

By age twelve, when he wasn't in school, he worked pulling weeds for people for fifty cents a day. Once, after he had worked all day for the mailman's wife, she refused to pay him. She told him she would give him some old clothes instead of the money. Astor didn't want her rags. He was hurt to have been lied to and to feel that he couldn't trust even the grown-ups in his own town. Astor felt that being mistreated this way was why some of the boys in town behaved badly.

One of Astor's favorite memories illustrates both the meagerness of his childhood in terms of material goods and the love he did receive. When he was about ten years old, he visited his father. He was riding along while his dad worked, hauling livestock and milk. At the end of the ride, his father handed him two Hershey bars. The boy had never had a Hershey bar in his life. During the Depression in Iowa, a candy bar was as good as a birthday present. Astor was thrilled, but he ate only one. The generous boy brought the second candy bar home and gave it to his foster mother. His foster parents were always good to him, he felt. Astor lived with his foster family until he turned eighteen and enlisted in the Army. He was patriotic and happy to serve. "We had a war to win," he believed.

Astor enlisted on February 5, 1944, in Des Moines, and by April, he was inducted and sent to one of the largest training sites in the world, Camp Roberts in Central California. This small-town boy was a part of something big now. More than 40,000 other soldiers were at the camp; the parade grounds were the length of fourteen football fields; and famous entertainers put on shows for the boys at the camp's Soldier's Bowl arena. The troops at Camp Roberts trained in infantry or artillery, to be replacements for troops who had been killed or injured and to fight in Operation Downfall, and Astor was assigned to the artillery. Although his training was very intense – only one day off in seventeen weeks – he noticed that the infantry training was even tougher. He admired those "dough boys," as he called them, using the World War I nickname for soldiers.

After training, Astor shipped out to Leyte and arrived there just as the fierce Battle for Leyte was winding down and the dangerous period of "mopping up" had begun – the U.S. had forced the Japanese troops to retreat, but some Japanese soldiers continued to fight. They hid in the jungles and attacked U.S. soldiers with sniper fire. Astor was in dangerous territory, and he appreciated the intensive training he had received back home.

Once most of the Japanese snipers had been taken out and Leyte was secured, Astor could focus more on his work, preparing for Operation Downfall. His job was to help get vehicles ready. Used trucks, jeeps and other vehicles had been shipped over from the War in Europe, which had just ended, and Astor would inspect the vehicles, load the ones that would run with ammunition, and drive them over to the airbase. The notion of invading Japan was unnerving. Astor had seen and heard enough about the fierce Japanese soldiers to be extremely worried about an invasion. Operation Downfall was expected to be a bloodbath. When Astor heard that the Japanese had finally surrendered, he was enormously relieved, like many others. He truly felt that his and countless other lives had been saved.

Astor's problem now was that he had not earned enough points to get discharged from the service. Astor had only thirty points, and at this point, the Army was discharging soldiers at the sixty-point level. Astor was worried that he would be sent to Japan to help in the post-war occupation that

MacArthur was leading. Astor didn't want to go to Japan even during peacetime. He figured that most Japanese hated Americans, the people who had devastated their country.

Sergeant Astor's story concludes in the next chapter.

People celebrated the world over when the war ended. Navy photographer Lt. Victor Jorgensen shot this photo in New York City's Times Square on August 14, 1945. Jorgensen shot this photo at the same time as a Life Magazine photographer named Alfred Eisenstaedt captured these two people on his camera, from a slightly different angle.
Photo courtesy of the U.S. National Archives, no. 80-G-377904.

24

Coming Home – The Rest of the Story

Sergeant James Astor

Astor, like most soldiers, had been advised by his buddies never to volunteer for anything in the Army – you just never knew what would be in store for you if you did – but Astor heard of a program that sounded pretty good and that would prevent him from going to Japan. The government had come out with an enlistment program. The American public was loudly demanding that the millions of U.S. troops overseas be demobilized and returned home, but the U.S needed servicemen and women for post-war occupation and other work, so it established enticements for troops to continue to serve.

Astor took advantage of the enlistment program, getting mustering-out pay, and for the remainder of his time in Leyte, he didn't have to wear a uniform or undergo inspections. He enjoyed wearing civilian clothes in Leyte, especially when he and his buddies went out. The locals were sick of the war and were tired of looking at soldiers. Astor took his sixty days of leave back in his hometown working for a farmer named Bates. Bates had a daughter named Laura Mae, and she became Astor's girlfriend.

After his leave, Astor eventually ended up at Camp Hood in Texas, working as a prison guard at the U.S. Disciplinary Barracks, which held U.S. troops who had broken the law. The temperature reached at least one hundred degrees every day, and of course there was no air conditioning. The prison was pretty miserable.

More than a thousand prisoners were held in a barracks, and the worst of the criminals were held in single cells. Ironically, it was during this work, after the war, when Astor felt most in danger. He had never felt so scared, every single day, in his entire life. The prisoners – some of whom were murderers and rapists – seemed as if they would just as soon as shoot you as look at you, Astor felt. The prisoners yelled at the guards as they patrolled the barracks and staged riots, attacked guards and set fires. The prisoners would get drunk from liquor they made, getting ahold of yeast from the kitchen, mixing it with fruit or juice and allowing it to ferment. They buried their concoctions so the guards couldn't find them, though the guards mainly stayed outside of the barracks.

Laura Mae and Astor wrote letters to each other. She wanted to visit him at Camp Hood, but Astor explained that it was no place for a young girl -- she was a senior in high school at the time. The men at Camp Hood were not goody good guys, he told her.

One day, a few of Astor's buddies from the Philippines took him aside and asked him to speak to the Inspector General of the camp. It turned out that some records had been mishandled and men were getting discharged ahead of Astor and his buddies when they should not have been. Astor's friends wanted him to speak for the group, even though Astor didn't know what he would say other than to go in and swear at the guy. Instead, Astor respectfully pointed out the error to his superior, and the next day he and his buddies were at the top of the list to be discharged.

Astor went home to Iowa and his girlfriend, and they were married in 1946, after Astor listened to Laura Mae's father's lectures about marriage. He was fond of his father-in-law, though, and helped him out on his farm.

Astor worked some tough jobs—in a poultry plant and a meat-cutting plant – and for a while paid rent to sleep on the kitchen floor of a friend's house to try to find better work in Cedar Rapids. His friend had five kids, so it was loud and hot in the kitchen where Astor stayed, but he did find work at a steel company. He moved his wife and the first of their five children to Cedar Rapids in their thirteen-year old De Soto, an enormous old car, and the family lived in a motel room until they could afford to buy a trailer. It took a while to move a poor family in 1950, Astor recalls.

He supported his family the old-fashioned way, saving his money and not getting into debt. Astor took a job at the Iowa Manufacturing Company, which made rock crushers, pavers and other equipment for building roads. It was a good job: U.S. President Dwight D. Eisenhower – former Allied Supreme Commander in the war – had made revitalizing the nation's roads one of his chief goals when he took office in 1953, and the Interstate Highway Act was passed a few years later. Road building was good business.

The kids helped around the house, and on Sundays the family all attended church together. Eventually, they saved enough to buy a larger trailer, then another one that was larger still, and finally they bought a house. Astor worked at Iowa Manufacturing for forty-one years, retiring in 1991. Laura Mae died in 2003, and he still misses her. Astor's children and grandchildren, nieces and nephews, all grew up to be good citizens, and he is proud of that. Now age eighty-nine, he's never forgotten what it felt like to have to leave home at the age of three. He is grateful that his family has come a long way since then.

Astor's awards include the Asiatic Pacific Campaign Medal and the Good Conduct Medal.

Sergeant Edwin Holopainen

Holopainen was going home on leave, expecting to return to war, when he heard the news that Japan had surrendered. He and his crew were on a ship somewhere between Hawaii and Seattle at the time. As Holopainen recalls, the men on the ship did not celebrate. They were happy to be going home and relieved that they would not have to return. They had just fought a brutal war, and they grieved the loss of so many of their brothers.

After the war, Holopainen returned to the family farm. Eleven boys in his town had died in the war, and he had known most of them. He married a girl named Pauline – they had attended Templeton High School together – and took a job in a factory that made industrial equipment. He and his wife lived with his family and saved their money. By 1950, they had saved enough to buy a piece of land and build a house. Holopainen hired a contractor to build most of it, and then he and his father finished it. Holopainen and his wife raised two daughters, Kristen and Jane, in their home.

Pauline had attended Becker Business College during the war and when their daughters were grown, she became the town clerk and tax collector for Templeton. Holopainen worked at the factory for forty years, supporting his family. When he retired, the company held a dinner for him and awarded him with a watch.

Despite all he endured as a young man, Holopainen thinks young people today have a harder time than he did. "You can't buy a house and raise a family with a working class job today. It's so much harder for young people to get their start today," Holopainen believes.

Holopainen is pleased that his grandsons have always been interested in what he did in the war. He's taken them to see a real B-29 bomber, though not the one he flew on. That was destroyed when it went down with another crew. The crew survived the crash. Years later, at an Air Force reunion, Holopainen and some of his former crewmates met that crew and teased them about destroying their plane.

Holopainen does not like to be called a hero. He says that the men who were captured and the ones who died were the true heroes. He would like people to understand that the firebombing and atomic bombing of Japan were absolutely necessary and saved hundreds of thousands of lives in the long run because they eliminated the need to attack the Japanese mainland in Operation Downfall. "The front line of combat in the invasion was expected to be two-hundred and fifty miles long. Hundreds of thousands of U.S. and Japanese would have been killed or wounded. It would have made D-Day look like a picnic," Holopainen explains.

Holopainen's awards include the Distinguished Flying Cross, the Asiatic-Pacific Theater Ribbon with Three Battle Stars, the Air Medal with Three Oak Leaf Clusters and the Good Conduct Medal.

First Class Aviation Machinist Mate Fran Phelps

When the war ended, the Training Center where Phelps worked was closed, and Phelps was sent to a Navy training base now called Naval Air Station Pensacola, located in Pensacola, Florida. "It was exciting when the war ended. Lots of girls got out, but I loved my job, so why leave? I planned to stay on as a career," Phelps recalls. Her plans changed when she met her future husband, Richardson Phelps, Jr., a graduate of the U.S. Naval Academy, Class of 1943, when he came through her office in Pensacola. He had served aboard a destroyer in the war and was training to fly in Pensacola. WAVES were not permitted to marry men in the Navy, so Phelps had to choose between marriage and career.

She resigned from the Navy after four years in the WAVES, but did not really leave the service. Phelps' husband's career was in the Navy – he eventually retired as a Commander – so Phelps was an officer's wife for more than twenty years, taking on and enjoying immensely the important social duties of that role. She stayed involved in the WAVES unofficially too. "At holidays, there were always a lot of WAVES at the house," she recalls.

Phelps wants to get a message out. "I want people to know that women played a very, very important part in saving this country during World War II," she says.

One prominent WAVES member was Grace Murray Hopper, who had earned her Ph.D. in Mathematics before the war and worked at a wartime computer project at Harvard University. After the war, she joined the Harvard faculty and retired from the Navy with the rank of Rear Admiral. Hopper is one of the mothers of computer science and is credited with co-inventing one of the first widely used computer languages, COBOL, and coining the term "computer bug." One of the first Navy ships named for a woman was the *USS Hopper* (DDG 70), which the Navy commissioned in 1997.

Two women in particular, who were not WAVES, made immeasurable contributions in intelligence during the war. Agnes Meyer Driscoll was a career cryptologist who worked for the Navy as a civilian during the war and was able to break into almost all of the Japanese naval codes the Navy worked on. The work of another woman, Genevieve Grotjan Feinstein, has been described by the U.S. National Security Agency as having "changed the course of history."

During the war, Japanese diplomats used a coding device known in U.S. intelligence as the "Purple Machine." In September of 1940, Feinstein, a mathematician who worked in the Army's Signal Intelligence Service, broke into the Purple code. This stunning achievement gave the U.S. access to Japanese diplomatic correspondence throughout the entire course of the war.

Phelps and her husband raised five children – Anne, Anthony, David, Sam and Joseph --in Falls Church, Virginia, a suburb of Washington, D.C.

Phelps was most likely the only mom in the neighborhood who fixed her own car and helped her kids build a dune buggy. "One time we took this VW that had been rolled and took the body off. We used a can opener to get most of it off. My son David was good with electronics, so he disabled the electrical system and sketched out how it was set up. We ordered a fiberglass body from California and bolted it onto the engine and put it all together. It was a dune buggy. It was the cutest little thing. My son Tony took it to college with him, and we called it 'the chick magnet,'" Phelps recalls. She was assistant, project manager and the biggest cheerleader as the kids built their car.

Phelps and her husband had planned to live aboard a sailing yacht after he retired, but those plans changed when one of their adult sons, Sam, was injured when a drunk driver ran into his car. The couple and Sam moved to Wilsonville, Alabama, where Phelps' extended family lived. After Phelps' son recovered, she became very active in local politics and was elected mayor of her small town twice, serving for eight years.

At age ninety-one, Phelps, whose husband died in 2007, is more energized than people half her age, and she is very active in a number of organizations. In 2014, she drove to Birmingham, Alabama, for the National Veterans' Day weekend of festivities, the oldest and often the largest Veterans' Day celebration in the U.S. Former U.S. Senator Bob Dole was honored, and many important people were in attendance. "There was a lot of brass there," Phelps recalls. She sat at the head tables at many of the banquets and functions and discussed issues with political acquaintances such as a member of President Obama's Cabinet – Deputy Secretary of Veterans Affairs Sloan D. Gibson, as well as U.S. Senator Jeff Sessions, U.S. Congressman Spencer Bachus (who had sworn her in as mayor), and Thomas C. Smith, the Director of the V.A. hospital in Birmingham. "I've always been involved in politics up to my ears," Phelps explains.

Phelps discusses veterans' issues with the politicians she knows. She is particularly concerned with V.A. medical care, and one issue she finds very important is the lack of space in V.A. hospitals for veterans with dementia or Alzheimer's Disease. "There aren't that many beds for veterans who have dementia and need around the clock care. Career military people only have the V.A. If someone like me got dementia, I would wind up out on the street. I'd run through my savings pretty fast in a private nursing home, and if there was no bed for me in a V.A. hospital, I would have nowhere to go," Phelps explains. Phelps also sits on the Stakeholder's Board of the Birmingham V.A. hospital. "It's a great hospital, and I want us to make all the V.A. hospitals as good as Birmingham," Phelps explains.

In 2012, Phelps flew to Washington, D.C., on an Honor Flight for World War II veterans. U.S. Senator Bob Dole and congressmen from Alabama met her group at the National World War II Memorial.

Phelps also works as a silver haired legislator. "Every state has a silver haired legislature. It's modeled on the regular legislature. We have general sessions and committees, and you represent the area where you live. We deal with senior citizens' needs, and my main focus is on veterans. We take our resolutions, debate them in committees and then encourage the regular legislators to turn them into bills and present them to the governor," Phelps explains.

Phelps' schedule includes many public speaking engagements. She particularly enjoys a teachers' ambassadors program, where veterans tell schoolteachers about their personal experiences, so that the teachers have their perspectives to pass along to their students. She also enjoys speaking to groups of girls who are thinking of going into the service.

Phelps says that staying active keeps her alive. She cooks food to bring to shut-ins and the elderly and admits with a laugh that some of those elderly people she serves are young enough to be her children. At age ninety-one, she flew as a passenger in a friend's restored Boeing-Stearman biplane, a type of plane she worked on in the war. "As we were coming in to land, my friend nosed the plane up, and we did a roll!" Phelps says with a laugh, adding, "I've had a fun time. Still am."

Phelps' awards include the American Theater Campaign Medal and the World War II Victory Medal.

After World War II ended, women were given a permanent role in the Navy when Congress passed the Women's Armed Services Integration Act in 1948, and the WAVES was disbanded, though the name continued to be used. In 1972, after the Women's Liberation Movement of the 1960's and 1970's, the Chief of Naval Operations set out guidelines to "equitably include women in our one-Navy concept," with the "ultimate goal, assignment of women to ships at sea." The Navy reached that goal in 1978.

Petty Officer Bob Poole

When the Japanese surrendered, Poole was off the coast of China aboard *The USS Alaska*. He remembers *The Alaska* taking Japanese prisoners from China back to Japan: "we treated the prisoners nicely," he recalls. *The Alaska* set out for home in November of 1945, and Poole steamed to Pearl Harbor, then to California, and back through the Panama Canal and to Boston, where he arrived on December 18, 1945. The *Alaska* went on to Bayonne New Jersey. She was awarded three battle stars, and her fate was to be placed on reserve and later decommissioned and scrapped. Poole's fate was to marry "the girl next door," raise four daughters together and work at an automotive and then an electronics factory. He is "as happy as a lark" living with his wife Shirley today. "When I think about the things I did, I'm so glad I'm still alive," he exclaims.

The *Tuscaloosa's* fate was to be decommissioned in 1946 and scrapped in 1959. Her mast is on display at the Tuscaloosa Veterans Park in Tuscaloosa, Alabama.

Poole's awards include the World War II Victory Medal and the Good Conduct Medal.

Sergeant Lawrence ("Bud") Dunn

After he had recovered from the illnesses and malnutrition he had contracted in the POW camps, Dunn spent a few days in Paris before flying home to the U.S. in a thunderstorm. He was sent home on a transport with other POWs. It was a very rough flight and Dunn thought how ironic it would have been if he and the others had survived so much only to go down on a plane after the war. Dunn landed on U.S. soil, in New York, on June 17, 1945. He couldn't wait to see his girlfriend, Aldine. "We had a date seventy-one years ago. I didn't want to get married before the war because that wouldn't have been fair, so she waited for me and then we got married," Dunn explains.

When Dunn was taken prisoner, the Germans took the prize wristwatch he had won in the basketball championships. After he returned home, his overjoyed family bought him a new watch.

After the war, Dunn worked for the U.S. Postal Service until he retired after thirty years. At age ninety, Dunn says happily that he has been married to "the most lovely woman in the world" for more than sixty-five years and that looking at her is the highlight of his day. The Dunns raised two sons, Larry and Bob, whom Dunn described in his journal as "two of the greatest people I have ever known." The Dunns are proud and doting grandparents and great grandparents.

Dunn's fingers still get numb easily from cold air, and the knee he ruptured when he was shot down is still painful for him, despite the three surgeries he has had over the years. While he never recovered enough to walk the golf course, this positive thinker looks at that situation as a reason to appreciate golf carts. Regarding his brutal treatment as a POW, Dunn wrote in his journal that, "Most POWs carry scars to this day. Mine are well hidden." Three of Dunn's friends died aboard his plane when it was attacked. Dunn has never forgotten these men and still has "heartbreaking" flashbacks of them lying dead in the plane.

Dunn did not apply for many of his awards until just recently. In 2014, he was in the process of filing for the Purple Heart Award, to which he is entitled for the injury to his knee. He is also entitled to certain POW awards. A few years before, Dunn's granddaughter Robin interviewed him for a high school project and asked him why he had waited for decades to apply for his medals. "I didn't need any more medals to tell me that I served in the Army and suffered many hardships. I just wanted to get home and forget about it all," Dunn told his granddaughter. Dunn ended his journal with the following words:

> If you have now traced the key points of my journey, don't cry for me. I am home where I belong and I am a very happy person.

Dunn's awards to date include the Air Medal with Three Oak Clusters, the European-African-Middle East Service Medal and the Good Conduct Medal. Dunn's squadron earned a Distinguished Unit Citation for the mission on which Dunn was shot down.

Private First Class Salvatore Santoro

More than seventy years later, Santoro still marvels at the fact that he asked to be drafted. "When I think about what I did, I almost can't believe it. I could have gotten malaria or gotten gassed to death," he exclaims. He had served in the National Guard from 1932 to 1935, and was entitled to longevity pay, which of course he wanted. His deployment was delayed while the Army confirmed his National Guard service, and that delay kept Santoro from actual combat. He considers himself very lucky.

After the war, the U.S. implemented elaborate plans for stabilizing Germany and restoring civilized life. Santoro stayed in Germany after the war for several months. He worked in public safety, and his job was to conduct spot raids on people's homes, with orders to impound any weapons, explosives, narcotics or radio transmitters found in civilian hands. He describes the Germans as "a good people," and says, "It amazes me that they fell for Hitler's baloney. They're very smart. We would never have gone to space without Werner von Braun, a German."

After several months of post-war work, Santoro was honorably discharged from the Army. He then worked for almost thirty years as an accountant with a Boston newspaper. Never forgetting how he had suffered during the Depression, he worked two jobs. "I took a civil service job too, so I have two pensions," he explains. Santoro has always been careful with his money. He did his banking at the East Boston Savings Bank for many years, liked the way the bank was run, and told the manager to let him know if the bank ever went "public," that is, if the bank decided to issue stock to the public so people like Santoro could invest in the bank. When the bank went public, Santoro bought shares and has doubled his money. His stockbroker is impressed.

"I watch my money. I've never owed money to anyone *ever,*" says Santoro. "I see people on T.V., saying they owe $30,000 or $40,000 dollars. They're out of their minds! If you can't afford a house or a vacation, then don't buy it; don't take it," cautions this survivor.

Santoro was married to his wife Eleanor for seventy-three years, until she died in 2012 at age ninety-seven. They raised two daughters and one son and then enjoyed travelling the world together – never borrowing a penny to do so, of course.

Santoro's awards include the Victory Medal, the European Theater Medal and the Good Conduct Medal.

Sergeant Bill Cooke

Later in the war, after Cooke had moved on, interrogations at P.O. Box 1142 focused less on questioning U-boat crews and more on interrogating German scientists, many of whom were famous in their fields of study. Wehrner von Braun, known as the father of rocket science, was interrogated at P.O. Box 1142. After the war, he went to work for the U.S. government and became one of the top leaders of the U.S. Army's rocket programt. Many preeminent German scientists went on to work in the U.S. after the war, mostly as a part of a project known as Operation Paperclip.

Cooke stayed in Manila, working, until the beginning of 1946, a few months after the war ended. Once he had the communications system up and running and had trained locals to operate it, his mission was accomplished. The Americans and Filipinos worked together to repair the destruction wrought by the war. The U.S. helped in this way all over the world.

When Cooke returned to the U.S., he brought home a grass skirt and an appreciation of very different cultures. He had met Midwesterners, Southerners, Germans, Pacific Islanders and more. He had witnessed the death and destruction of war. He had helped rescue and rebuild a grateful nation. Like the millions of others who served, he had experienced the world in a way he never would have but for the war. As many people had predicted, Americans' lives would never be the same.

Cooke was discharged from the Army on February 26, 1946, after three years of service to his country. During the war, he had sent his paychecks home to his father to pay for a new car, so he bought himself a beautiful, 1946 Mercury Sedan-Coupe. Cooke graduated from college and went on to a very successful career in sales and purchasing in the aerospace industry. He sometimes worked with German aerospace engineers who had moved to the U.S. after the war and with regard to them, Cooke has a postscript to his work at P.O. Box 1142.

As a part of his job in the aerospace industry, Cooke took scientists with whom he worked to his company's headquarters in Alabama. "These guys would stay with me awhile, and then they would peel off to go to Huntsville to the Space Center, to see Werner Von Braun. They all knew him. He brought a lot of his people with him after the war," Cooke explains.

Cooke married his wife Evelyn in 1951, and together they raised two daughters, Judy Ann and Mary-Beth. It was "a devastating blow" when his wife died in 2011, after sixty years of marriage.

At age 91, Cooke paints beautiful tributes to the works of Norman Rockwell, the famous illustrator known for *The Saturday Evening Post* magazine covers. Cooke's stories about his war service are not unlike a Rockwell painting – patriotic to the core but always laced with a bit of sweet humor.

He remembers being jealous that the German prisoners got to go "out on the town" so interrogators could get them talking: "I was eighteen years old, working, and these prisoners were out having fun." He also ran into a bit of trouble while out joy riding with Filipino friends after the war had ended. A buddy at the motor pool got him out of the jam, and Cooke repaid him by giving him his monthly allotment of cigarettes, which Cooke, a non-smoker, normally used for trade. "I was a little bit of a hell raiser back then," he admits with a smile, "but I did get my Good Conduct medal."

In addition to the Good Conduct Medal, Cooke's awards include the Victory Medal, the Asiatic Pacific Theater Campaign Ribbon, the American Theater Campaign Ribbon and the Philippine Liberation Ribbon with Bronze Service Star. He also received two awards from the Philippine government: the Philippine Liberation Medal and the Philippine Republic Presidential Unit Citation. Cooke also received a Certificate of Appreciation from the National World War II Memorial in Washington, D.C.

Before and after World War II, P.O. Box 1142 was known as Fort Hunt, so named when the U.S. War Department constructed it as a garrison for the Spanish-American War. The War Department used Fort Hunt for many purposes over the years. In 1930, Fort Hunt was transferred to the predecessor to the National Park Service and was a part of the recreational land that visitors enjoyed when visiting Mount Vernon. The Army took it over at the outset of World War II and referred to it only by the code name P.O. Box 1142. One German prisoner held there reportedly recognized where he was – he had picnicked at Fort Hunt with friends before the war on a visit to the

States and a tour of Mount Vernon. Today, Fort Hunt is once again a pastoral picnic area, and a sign denotes its interesting history.

The U.S. established an intelligence base similar to P.O. Box 1142 in California to interrogate Japanese prisoners. Byron Hot Springs was located near San Francisco and also employed the Ritchie Boys and their top-notch techniques.

Captain Reed Bertolette

After the war, Bertolette flew missions over China, dropping food to former prisoners of war who had been left to starve when the Japanese guards fled the prisons. He was discharged from the service in November of 1945 and was married in 1951 to a girl named Martha, whom everyone called "Mops." Bertolette worked as a sales engineer in Illinois, North Carolina and in Connecticut, where he and his wife settled in 1962. They raised a daughter, Katharine, and two sons, Reed, Jr. and Russell. Bertolette's wife died in 2011.

Bertolette's awards include the Distinguished Service Cross, three Air Medals, the Asiatic Pacific Theater Medal and the Good Conduct Medal.

Sergeant Paul Boyer

After the Japanese surrendered in August of 1945, the Allies confiscated their weapons. While waiting for his discharge papers to be processed, Boyer was sent into a warehouse full of Japanese weapons "stacked like cordwood," he recalls, and told to pick out two "souvenirs." He selected an Imperial Japanese Army rifle and a small sword still in its scabbard, all of which he still has, seventy years later. He remembers the rifle sticking out of his duffle and clanging into walls on the ship that carried him home from the Pacific.

Boyer is an adept writer and had this to say about his war experience:

The country owes a great amount to the armed forces person-

nel for their courage and sacrifice. They gave their all. The home front produced quality arms, tanks, ships and aircraft in such large quantities that the service men and women had the equipment to defeat the Germans and Japanese. It can also be said it was a joint effort by all. We are a Great Nation.

After the war, President Harry Truman sent out a letter on White House stationery, thanking the troops for their service and addressing each recipient by name. The letter Boyer received reads as follows:

To you who have answered the call of your country and served in its Armed Forces to bring about the total defeat of the enemy, I extend the heartfelt thanks of a grateful Nation. As one of the Nation's finest, you undertook the most severe task one can be called upon to perform. Because you demonstrated the fortitude, resourcefulness and calm judgment necessary to carry out that task, we now look to you for leadership and example in further exalting our country in peace.

Boyer married his sweetheart, Mary, after the war. During the war Mary had worked for the Civil Public Service in the censorship department and afterwards worked as a teacher for twenty years. The couple settled in Norwich, Connecticut, and raised two sons, John and Peter. Boyer, who was widowed after sixty-three years of marriage, worked as an insurance claims adjuster for twenty-seven years. According to the folks at the Norwich V.F.W. Post 594, at age 90 Boyer is still a terrific golfer.

Boyer's awards include the World War II Victory Award, the Asiatic Pacific Campaign Award with Four Campaign Stars, the American Campaign Award, the Far East Air Force President Unit Citation and the Army Good Conduct Award. The Philippine government honored him with the Philippine Liberation Award. Boyer also wears a WW II 3 Years of Service Hash Mark and Four Overseas Bars, a U.S. Army Pacific Theater Badge, an Air Force Badge, a Far East Air Force Badge and Four Bars.

U.S. infantrymen fighting their way through Europe on September 7, 1944. Photographer Geddicks.
Photo courtesy of the U.S. National Archives, number 111-SC-193835.

Sergeant Bill Burrus

The 87th ended the war in Friedewald, Germany, having taken more than 10,000 German soldiers as prisoners. They had an area that they had fenced off for their prisoners. Many Germans wanted to surrender because they were afraid of being taken prisoner by the Russians. Burrus recalls that one day, a German general rode up on a bike to surrender. He had brought a bottle of wine with him as if it were a social occasion.

Burrus had a wonderful experience late in the war during a break in the fighting. He was sitting on a barrel, getting his hair cut by one of the other soldiers. A jeep pulled up and out strode General George S. Patton, wearing his signature cavalry pants and boots and carrying two pearl-handled revolvers at his hips. Generals had a lenient dress code, and this was Patton's preferred uniform. Patton was very strict about his men's discipline and appearance, so perhaps he took a shine to the boy getting his hair cut while on a break from fighting. The general walked right up to Burrus and hit him on the shoulder. He said, "We've got this war going strong, and we're going to win it." Then he hit him on the shoulder again, got back into his jeep and drove away.

Eisenhower wrote that the infantrymen show "real heroism, which is the uncomplaining acceptance of unendurable conditions." Burrus and his fellow soldiers were truly heroes.

After the Germans surrendered in May and the War in Europe ended, the 87th was sent back to the U.S. The Golden Acorn Division was preparing to fight in the Pacific when Japan surrendered and the war ended.

Burrus' luck continued to hold out, and the end of the war found him promoted to Technical Seargent working on Governor's Island outside of New York City, at a Women's Army Corps barracks. He made friends with a woman there who was a singer in New York, and the couple enjoyed all the best places to party in Manhattan. "New York City treated us like royalty," Burrus says, referring to his fellow veterans. Burrus and his friend went dancing a lot, and Burrus still enjoys dancing. While stationed in New York, Burrus waited to be redeployed to Japan and was relieved that Operation Downfall was cancelled.

Burrus thought about reenlisting, but his mother was upset with the idea, so he decided against it. Burrus moved back to Birmingham soon after the war when his father became ill. After his father died, he helped take care of his mother and his brother, who had been severely injured during basic training for the war and was bedridden for more than forty years in the family's home, until he died at age 63. Like the Burrus family, many people suffered privately from the war for years and years.

Burrus married and raised one daughter and three sons. He has been married to his second wife, Ercelle, for forty-four years. Burrus founded a financial services agency fifty years ago and still works there every day at age 89. "My clients are my friends now, so I don't want to walk away from that," he explains. Burrus was bashful as a kid, so he took a Dale Carnegie public speaking class after the war and was an instructor for fourteen years. He also enjoyed having his pilot's license and buying and selling planes for many years.

Burrus never picked up a rifle again after the war, but someone gave him a fancy pistol and he enjoys shooting that at the range. He and Ercelle spend all the holidays with their children, grandchildren and great-grandchildren, the ninth of whom was just born. He and Ercelle have a wonderful time with their family. "It's my decision as to whether I have a good day or a bad day. We're all going to have problems. It's how you confront them that matters," he advises.

Burrus attended college and law school after the war. When he was drafted and pulled out of high school, he had wanted to serve in the Air Corps but was ineligible because the Army had pulled him out before graduation. Later, his high school gave him credit for his military training and service. One day in Europe during a lull in the fighting, Burrus was in a pup tent and heard a mail call. He had received an envelope from back home. In it was his high school diploma. He had graduated with the class of 1945.

Looking back at all his life's experiences, Burrus says, "It's been a good run, honey."

Burrus's awards include the World War II Victory Medal, the World War II Europe Africa Campaign Medal, the American Campaign Medal, the Presidential Unit Citation, the Combat Infantry Badge, the Army Marksman Badge (Rifle), the Army Expert Shooting Badge (Machine Gun), and the Good Conduct Award.

Carpenter's Mate Joe Vendola

America's presence in Newfoundland changed many lives. There were some negative aspects, certainly. The U.S. depopulated the entire town of Argentia to build the base, so people were forced to move out of homes that had been in their families for generations. Some had to be forcibly removed. While the U.S. compensated the owners of the two hundred homes, many locals felt that the compensation was inadequate. The U.S. also exhumed three cemeteries to make room for the base.

Overall, however, the U.S. presence in Newfoundland was overwhelmingly positive. The economic boom during the war took Newfoundland from deficit spending to a surplus, and in 1942, mandatory, free public schooling for all the children in the country was established. After the war, the U.S. and Canada, who also had a significant presence in the country, left behind a vast, modern infrastructure of airports, railroads, paved roads, electrical grids, communication lines and hospitals. This was no longer a backward fishing island.

The culture on the island had shifted away from Britain and more toward North America. After the war, with Newfoundland's economy strengthened and England's power weakened, Newfoundland was able to free itself of British dominion and join Canada.

The shipwreck and its aftermath in Newfoundland had a tremendous impact on Lanier Phillips. Up until then, he understandably felt bitter about his lot in life. That feeling, combined with the limited opportunities for African Americans in the U.S., did not seem to be the basis for a very rewarding future for this young man. Experiencing the extraordinary self-sacrifice and kindness from the people who saved him changed Phillips' life forever. He had never known that white people could treat black people like equal human beings. Phillips said, quite beautifully, that the experience erased all of his hate.

After the war ended, Phillips challenged the policies that barred his advancement in the service and became the Navy's first black sonar technician. He had an acclaimed career as a deep-sea specialist and worked with Jacques Cousteau, the leading deep sea explorer of the century. Phillips also went on to become an important civil rights leader, lecturing around the U.S. and marching with Dr. Martin Luther King.

In 2010, the U.S. Navy Memorial awarded Phillips the Lone Sailor Award, one of the organization's highest awards. The award recognizes Navy veterans who have distinguished themselves in their civilian work while embodying the Navy's central values of honor, courage and commitment.

Civil rights leaders worked for equal treatment for black troops and other minorities throughout the war, but not much changed until after the war ended. On October 29, 1947, President Truman's Committee on Civil Rights recommended that the U.S. "end immediately all discrimination and segregation based on race, color, creed or natural origin in…all branches of the U.S. government."

Over the years since the war, Vendola and Phillips wrote letters to each other, they talked on the phone from time to time, and they finally met in person in the spring of 2007, when Vendola's son and daughter in-law took him to Washington, D.C. Also, Vendola met with Bergeron, the hero who hiked along that fence in the snow, several times over the years since the war. Bergeron died in 2010. Phillips died in 2012, leaving Vendola the last living survivor of the *Truxtun*.

After the war, Vendola returned home to Norwich, Connecticut, and worked as a machinist throughout his career. He and his wife raised a daughter, Linda, and a son, Thomas, and have been married for 65 years. He is forever grateful to the people of St. Lawrence for risking their lives to save him and his mates.

Vendola's awards include the Navy World War II Victory Medal, the Asiatic Pacific Campaign Medal with One Bronze Star, the European African Middle Eastern Campaign Medal, the Navy Good Conduct Medal, the American Defense Service Medal with a Bronze A, the American Campaign Medal, the Combat Action Ribbon and the Honorable Service Lapel Pin.

Vendola did not receive his awards until sixty-five years after his honorable discharge from the service. Robert A. Murphy, Vice Chair of the Norwich Area Veterans Council, learned in 2011 that Vendola had never received his medals. Murphy enlisted the help of Congressman Joe Courtney, and they applied for and obtained Vendola's awards. Vendola was presented with his medals at the Norwich VFW Post 594 in May of 2011, when he was 91 years old. The formal award ceremony for Vendola included a flag line of the post's unit of Young Marines and attendance by the Patriot Guard Council Riders. Congressman Courtney personally presented the medals to Vendola. It was a proud day for America.

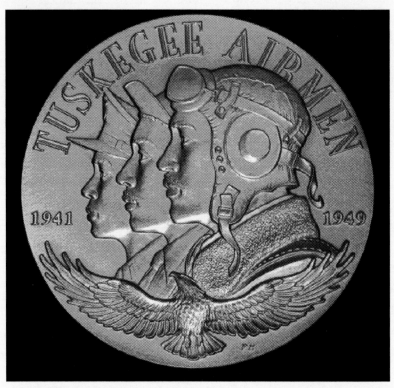

U.S. Air Force photograph of the Congressional Gold Medal awarded to the Tuskegee Airmen.

Colonel Harry Stewart

The "Red Tails," as the Tuskegee Airmen came to be known, have been depicted in books and films and are a source of myth and legend. One myth is that they never lost a bomber, and while that myth has been dispelled, it is not completely unfounded – they had many victories. The 332nd Fighter Group earned approximately sixty Purple Heart awards, fourteen Bronze Stars, three Distinguished Unit Citations, including the two awarded to the 99th Fighter Squadron, and ninety-six Distinguished Flying Crosses.

A third all-black unit, the 477th Bombardment Group, which did not see combat, also trained at Tuskegee. The Group was stationed for a time at Freeman Field, Illinois, and in April of 1945 – the same month Stewart earned the Distinguished Flying Cross – they staged a protest of racial discrimination at the base when black officers were denied admission to the officers' club.

Stewart returned home after the war, in October of 1945. "I stayed in the Air Force four more years because I loved the flying," he explains. In March of 1948, he was on maneuvers in a P-47 fighter when his engine failed, and he had to bail out, parachuting down about 100 yards from the home of the West family in Butcher Hollow, in Johnson County, Kentucky, and breaking his leg in two places. The West family included a thirteen-year-old daughter who would go on to become the famous country singer and songwriter, Loretta Lynn. She sang often about her home in Butcher Hollow, which became a tourist destination. Unbeknownst to Stewart, wild rumors based on his bailout became a part of the legend of Butcher Hollow.

In 2005, Stewart received a completely unexpected phone call from an historian. He wanted to ask Stewart about his experience landing in Butcher Hollow back in 1948. The historian explained the story as he had heard it: after the war, a black man stole a B-52 from the U.S. Air Force, and U.S. Air Force fighter planes chased after him, shot him down, and he landed in Butcher Hollow, just outside of the little mining town of Van Lear. When Stewart heard this outlandish story, he laughed so hard he almost fell out of his chair. "The B-52 is an extremely complicated jet that takes a large crew to fly," Stewart explains. A person can't just come along and steal a Boeing B-52 Stratofortress. Another problem with the far-fetched story -- the B-52 hadn't even been manufactured yet – it first flew four years after Stewart's bail out, on April 15, 1952. Stewart and the historian had a good laugh and the historian published an accurate account of the bailout. As a result, Stewart recalls, "A couple of years later, the town invited me to visit and had me serve as Parade Marshal in the town parade. I stayed four or five days, visited the West family's cabin and Loretta Lynn's brother gave me a tour. It was a very nice visit."

In May of 1949, not long before Stewart retired from active duty and joined the reserves, the Air Force held its first Top Gun meet, outside of Las Vegas, Nevada. (The Army Air Corps had held gunnery meets prior to the war, but this was the first meet of the newly formed, independent military branch, the U.S. Air Force.) The all-black 332nd Fighter Group was invited to send a team of pilots, and Group Commander Col. Benjamin Davis reportedly told the three-man team, "If you don't win, don't come back." There would be two winners – one team from the new jet engine class and one team from the conventional piston engine class. The competitors scored points in aerial gunnery, dive bombing, skip bombing, rocket firing and strafing.

By the end of the first day of the two-day competition, Stewart's team had both the highest team score and the highest individual score, flying in the piston-engine class. In skip bombing, for instance, the pilot flies very low to the ground and releases the bomb so that it falls flat to the ground and skips along to the target. In the skip bombing portion of the meet, Stewart scored six out of six, as did his teammates Capt. Alva Temple and Lt. Col. James Harvey. In rocket firing on the second day of the meet, Temple scored six out of six, and Stewart and Harvey got five out of six. In the end, the Tuskegee Airmen's team won its class.

The trophy from that first meet, bearing the names of Stewart and his teammates, is on display at the National Museum of the U.S. Air Force at Wright Patterson Air Force Base, near Dayton, Ohio.

Soon after the Top Gun meet, Stewart left active duty and "decided to take the corporate route," he explains. He moved back to New York City with his wife, Delphine, whom he had married a couple years earlier. "I met my wife through her brother. I flew with him – he was a fighter pilot too. We were on leave, and I went to his house and met her. We courted for fifteen months and married in January of 1947," he explains.

Stewart enrolled in New York University and graduated with a Bachelor's of Science degree in Mechanical Engineering. He advanced steadily through the ranks of corporate America, from the engineering department of General Foods, to the Bechtel Corporation, which is headquartered in San Francisco, California and is the largest construction and engineering company in the United States. He and his wife raised their daughter Lori in the area.

Stewart capped off his career as the Vice President of ANR Pipeline, then headquartered in Detroit, Michigan, which operates one of the largest natural gas pipeline systems in the U.S. In addition, "I maintained my reserve affiliation with the Air Force, with a two-week tour of duty each year, until I retired at age sixty," he explains.

In April of 2006, the U.S. Congress passed legislation awarding the Tuskegee Airmen the Congressional Gold Medal of Honor, the highest award that Congress can award to civilians. In 2007, Stewart and five of his fellow Tuskegee Airmen accepted the Congressional Gold Medal of Honor from President George W. Bush, who remarked, "even the Nazis asked why they would fight for a country that treated them unfairly." Stewart, though, had never let racial prejudice affect the happiness and fulfillment he found in flying and in serving his country. At age ninety, Stewart looks back at what he describes as "a very exciting life" and says, "I wouldn't have changed a single thing in the whole odyssey."

Stewart lives with his wife of sixty-seven years in the Detroit area. "I've had a very exciting life," he says, adding, "I have no complaints, just gratitude."

Stewart's awards include the Distinguished Flying Cross, the Air Medal with Seven Oak Leaf Clusters, the Distinguished Unit Citation, the Victory Medal, and the European Theater Campaign Ribbon.

Gunner's Mate Rudy Rolenz

After the war, Rolenz returned to the States on a troop ship by way of Pearl Harbor, landed in California, took a train out east and was discharged at the Great Lakes Naval Station. He went home to his parents. Rolenz had three brothers who lived until adulthood, and they all served too. A younger brother served in Korea and two others served in World War II.

"My older brother served aboard the *USS Savannah* in the European Theater. He was a radio operator. One night he was working in the fantail of the ship, and another operator who was in the counting tower asked to change watches with him. My brother agreed. The next thing that happened, the ship got bombed and the other guy got killed. My brother never got over it," Rolenz explains sadly.

Rolenz' brother Emil served in the U.S. Army Signal Corps as an electrical engineer, "in the Pacific, setting up equipment for soldiers to use," Rolenz explains, and he went on to a career in the aerospace industry. It's hard to imagine how Rolenz' parents managed during the war with three sons in battle. Rolenz explains his family's service: "So we did our share for our country. That's what you're supposed to do." He thinks of his service as a very important part of his development as a person. "I wish our kids today had to serve. It teaches discipline and how to obey orders. It would teach the kids how to take care of themselves, their clothes and how to get themselves around and travel," Rolenz explains.

Over the years, Rolenz has enjoyed keeping up with the progress at the Amphibious Training Base at Little Creek, Virginia, which was a rustic, hardscrabble little base when he trained there. During the war, specialized demolition units that trained at Little Creek were the forerunners of today's Navy SEALs (Sea, Air, Land Teams). The Mercury astronauts received their amphibious training at Little Creek in the spring of 1959, as the nation announced its first mission into outer space.

Today, Little Creek, along with the neighboring Army Post Fort Story, is known as the Joint Expeditionary Base Little Creek – Fort Story. A joint base commanded by the Navy, it is the Army's central amphibious training base and widely considered to be the premier base of the U.S. Navy.

As far as that Navy hat that he wore all through the Pacific, Rolenz has for the most part kept his promise to never wear a hat again, even though he lives in Ohio, where the winters are rough. He might not have been the only soldier, sailor or marine who became sick of hats during the war. Wearing a formal hat everyday soon dropped out of fashion after the war ended.

Rolenz spent his career in the tire industry, meeting the woman he would marry at a buddy's wedding. He and Doris have been married almost 68 years and have two surviving sons and four grandchildren. Their son John, who worked as an electrician, died in an accident in 2007. Doris spent her career as a secretary with the local board of education. Doris never thought she would marry a Navy man. "I always said I would never go with a sailor because they had a girl in every port," Doris explains with a laugh. "I sure appreciate her," Rolenz says.

Rolenz's awards include the American Campaign Medal, the Asiatic-Pacific Campaign Medal with Three Bronze Stars, the World War II Victory Medal, the Philippine Liberation Medal and the Good Conduct Medal.

Petty Officer Buck Lord

After the war, Lord returned home to Texas. Before he left Guam, he wrote a series of letters to his wife Frankie and left them with a friend who mailed one every few days. That way he could surprise Frankie by returning home without her having known he was in transit, when he would be unable to send her letters. She always thought it was humorous that he had written "ahead of time." Lord says that they laughed about those letters many times, until Frankie died last year after seventy years of marriage.

Lord spent his career in retail sales, and he and Frankie raised two daughters, Debbie and Becky, who in turn had daughters. "We finally got some boys when the great grandkids came along," Lord explains. He took Frankie to visit Hawaii so she could get a feel for his life in the Pacific and they even considered living there once.

Today Apra Harbor is home to a U.S. Naval base and a large commercial port. More than fifty shipwrecks from the war remain underwater, and diving to explore them is a popular tourist activity. Memorials to the war can be found all over the island. A major memorial is the Asan Overlook, from which people can view Apra Harbor and the beaches where the U.S. Marines came ashore. That day, July 21, 1944, is still celebrated as Liberation Day and is a very important holiday in Guam.

Guam remains a U.S. territory and its tropical beauty attracts many tourists. As an indication that scars can heal, most vacationers who visit Guam come from Japan.

Lord's medals include the Bronze Star, the World War II Victory Award, the Asiatic-Pacific Campaign Award and the Navy Good Conduct Medal. The ship aboard which Lord worked, the *USS City of Dalhart*, earned a battle star for meritorious participation in battle.

Lieutenant Paul Lahr

Lahr and his crewmates – the same crew assigned together back in Rapid City, Iowa – continued to fly together after the war in a top-secret project. They were a part of what was essentially an early Cold War mission: the aerial mapping of nearly two million square miles of Europe and North Africa. The project was known as "Casey Jones," after the legendary railroad engineer from Tennessee who died while saving others in a railroad accident, and was one of the first major projects in what would become the critical military science of Manned Airborne Intelligence, Surveillance and Reconnaissance.

Lahr and his crewmates worked on Casey Jones until March of 1946, and Lahr was released from active duty on August 22, 1946. He stayed in the Reserves until May 29, 1959, when he retired with the rank of 1st Lieutenant. Lahr graduated with a B.S. in Chemistry from Syracuse University in 1950 and made his career in technical sales. At age 90, Lahr lives in New York State with his wife Jean, enjoys golf and gave up skiing just a few years ago. This survivor gets a chuckle out of reading that times are hard these days, saying, "I suppose it's all relative."

Lahr's awards include the World War II Victory Medal, the American Campaign Medal, the European African Middle Eastern Campaign Medal, the Army of Occupation Medal, and the Good Conduct Medal.

Captain Lois Crook

Crook was still in Victorville when the war ended, and the celebrations were huge. She wanted to stay in the service and was assigned to Luke Air Force Base outside Phoenix, Arizona. Her life would be transformed at Luke.

The work at Luke was more difficult because the hospital ward treated wounded soldiers, sailors and marines returning from the Pacific. Many had broken down mentally from the anguish they had witnessed in the war. Some of them had completely lost their minds and had to be kept in restraints. Many were badly scarred, wounded or disfigured. Though it was hard work and tough emotionally to treat and console her patients, Crook found her service to be deeply satisfying.

Luke was the largest fighter pilot training base in the country and was known as the "Home of the Fighter Pilot." One of these dashing pilots swept Crook right off her feet. One evening, in the fall of 1945, a girlfriend of Crook's, another nurse, asked her to join her on a blind date with two fighter pilots. The nurses all lived on base at the Nurses' Quarters, and the pilots lived at the Pilots' Quarters. Going on a date meant hanging out together at the Officers' Club.

The girlfriend's date was a tall, handsome fellow named Clyde Ray Jones, Jr. Jones was a Southern boy, born in Durham, North Carolina, and was one year to the month younger than Crook. He spoke with a sweet drawl, was smart and brave, as fighter pilots generally were, and he had a sense of ambition that matched Crook's. Jones and Crook couldn't keep their eyes off each other. The next day, he called her, and that was that. They were a couple. When Jones wasn't flying and Crook wasn't working in the hospital ward, they were inseparable. Then, they both had to leave Luke AFB.

Since the war had ended, the fighter pilots were training for non-combat roles. In the fall of 1946, one year after their blind date, Jones was sent to Georgia to train to be an Adjutant General, an administrative job. At around the same time, Crook was sent to Keesler Field near Biloxi, Mississippi. They wrote letters to each other to stay in touch. A couple of months later, in December, Jones wrote that he was on leave in Mobile, Alabama, visiting a friend and that he wanted to come to visit her. Crook requested a three-day leave, Jones and his buddy picked her up, and the three drove to Mobile for a long weekend.

While Jones and Crook checked into two separate rooms at a hotel, the buddy went to get his girlfriend, and then the foursome went out for an evening of dinner and dancing at an elegant nightclub. Since the war was over and she was not on duty, Crook was able to wear a pretty, teal blue suit instead of her uniform. The band played "Stars Fell Over Alabama," and

Crook felt starry. It was a beautiful, romantic evening.

Back at the hotel, Jones had to tell Crook some important news. He was being sent to Japan for a three-year tour of duty. The couple stayed up all night talking about the prospect of being apart for three years. The notion seemed unbearable. At some point during their marathon conversation, they decided to get married.

In the morning, Jones called his buddy, Lt. F.L. Christopher, and told him their news. Christopher stormed over to the hotel to try to talk him out of it. He spent at least two hours trying to convince Jones that this was a bad idea, repeating over and over, "You don't want to *do* this!" Jones and Crook just sat there, not saying much, just smiling happily, holding hands, and thinking about getting married. They had no idea of where or when it would happen, but they were going to be husband and wife before Jones left for Japan.

Finally Christopher gave up and told them, "Well, if you're going to get married, then I guess I'll have to help you." He pointed out that they needed to get married back in Mississippi because there was no waiting period for getting a license there and asked Crook for the name of a big hotel in Biloxi. All she could think of was the Biloxi Hotel, so he called there and told them to set up for a wedding that afternoon – he was bringing a couple over to get married there before the groom had to ship out for Japan.

During the war, many people got married like this, on a moment's notice, so the people at the hotel were not shocked. In fact, they were delighted. The hotel had been closed for repairs for three months and had just re-opened that very day. The hotel manager, Mrs. Freda Westbrook, took charge of the planning. She asked Christopher what religion the couple was and arranged for a Methodist minister to conduct the ceremony. She also called the local court clerk and arranged for him to meet the couple at the Marriage License Bureau, which he had to open because it was a Sunday.

Crook, Jones, Christopher and his girlfriend, Helen Glass, gathered their things and drove out to Biloxi. They arrived at the hotel to a flurry of activity, and the bride and groom were told to rush over to get their marriage license. When they returned with the license, they were told they had to be married immediately – the minister had to perform church services that evening.

The hotel had been beautifully decorated with flowers, and the hotel had corsages for the bridal party to wear. Crook and Jones were married in front of the fireplace. All of the hotel's guests and employees attended the ceremony, and when the couple was pronounced husband and wife, everyone cheered. Afterwards, the small wedding party enjoyed a candlelit, champagne dinner, and then husband and wife went off to the hotel's bridal suite, which also had been adorned with flowers. A local reporter had been called in to attend the spur-of-the-moment wedding, and he wrote an article about the event for the society section of the Biloxi Daily Herald.

It was a whirlwind, romantic thing to do, but they were ecstatic to be husband and wife. Several months later, in June of 1947, Crook, now a Captain in the Air Force, requested a discharge to begin married life with her new husband. Two years later, Crook gave birth to a healthy baby girl, whom they named Leslie. The couple was overjoyed with their baby, and they were madly in love. The little family moved around a lot, from base to base. During the spring of 1951, Jones worked at Eniwetok Atoll, located about 2,500 miles southwest of Honolulu. He worked in Operation Greenhouse, a highly secretive operation in which the U.S. conducted more than thirty nuclear explosions. Crook didn't know what her husband was involved with at Eniwetok because everyone in the operation signed very strict confidentiality agreements, but he did bring home a burned-out sign that said, "Greenhouse '51."

Crook had married a fighter pilot and that was dangerous work, but the war was over and she figured that now he had a safe, desk job. What many people did not realize at the time, however, was that when World War II ended, the Cold War began. The Cold War was an ideological dispute over whether the people of various nations of the world should be governed under democratic principles or under communism. Underlying the Cold War was the threat of a nuclear attack by the two global superpowers, which were mutual enemies in this war -- the U.S. and the U.S.S.R.

At the end of World War II, Korea was split into two countries. To the north of the 38th parallel of latitude, was North Korea, a communist state. South Korea was democratic. On June 25, 1950, North Korea invaded South Korea, and the U.S. decided to intervene on behalf of the democratic country in order to prevent the spread of communism. Jones was ordered to deploy for the conflict. He was to go back to war as a fighter pilot.

The little family of three moved to England, and Jones began training at the Royal Air Force Station Manston, located in Kent, about 100 miles southwest of London, where the U.S. Air Force based its Strategic Air Command during the 1950's. Jones was a part of the 123rd Fighter-Bomber Wing and trained on the F-84E Thunderjet. The Thunderjet was the second jet fighter used in the Air Force.

Jones loved flying, but he didn't like the idea of leaving his wife and child at home while he flew dangerous missions in the Korean War. He and Crook discussed his leaving the service when his commission ended. They researched many different colleges and universities and decided that they would attend the University of Mississippi, in Oxford, Mississippi. They didn't know anyone there, but Ole Miss seemed to be the perfect school, and they both had enjoyed Mississippi when Crook had been stationed there. Jones would study engineering, and Crook would get a bachelor's degree in science.

Jones received his orders: he would be leaving for Korea on February 9, 1953. Three days earlier, he wrote to his parents to tell them he was off to fight on a three-month tour. He wrote, "I don't mind going, it's just that I hate to leave Lois and Leslie for so long." Later that day, on February 6, Jones went up in his plane for one of his last scheduled practice sessions. Under the wings of his plane were loads of ammunition, so that he could get a feel for the weight he would be carrying on his missions. His was the second plane in a two-plane formation. Practice sessions were different from training sessions, in which unarmed pilots might encounter other planes and practice maneuvers or play aircraft tag, perfecting their maneuvering skills. While Jones was flying along, a pilot up on a training session misunderstood the situation and performed a mock attack on Jones. The other pilot, who was very accomplished, flew up behind Jones and accidentally clipped Jones' wing. The ammunition on Jones' plane exploded. Jones was killed.

Back in their little duplex, Crook was trying to prepare dinner, but she was nervous. Her husband was late coming home. At about six o'clock, the doorbell rang, and her blood ran cold. At the door were Jones' Commanding Officer and an Army Chaplain. Leslie waited in the kitchen for her mother, and when she didn't come back, the little girl walked over to the front door, where her mother was standing with her face buried in tissues. The Chaplain asked Crook if he should tell Leslie what happened, and Crook nodded her head.

Bending down on one knee, the Chaplain told Leslie that her daddy had died and gone up to heaven. Leslie could picture him floating up in the sky to heaven, but she didn't understand that she would never see her father again. Crook asked what had happened, but she was just told that her husband's plane had gone down in an accident and that he had been killed, along with the pilot of the other plane involved. The accident was being investigated.

That evening, Jones' wingman – the pilot of the other plane in his formation – came by to pick up Jones' uniform, and he told Crook that he saw the two planes going down in a cloud of black smoke. That was all Crook knew about the accident.

The Air Force was very efficient in getting Crook and her daughter packed up and moved out of their little house. In just a couple of days, Crook and her daughter were on a plane back to the U.S. The widow of the other pilot and her six-month-old baby son were on the plane with Crook. The Air Force wives always knew that early widowhood was highly likely for them, and they supported each other. Crook sat on the plane in a daze. She didn't even know the details of her husband's death. The love of her life was just gone.

For months, Crook would go over the accident in her mind, especially when she was trying to sleep. She would picture Jones getting into his plane, taking off and flying very fast – 400-500 miles per hour – up to 20,000 feet off the ground, and then, what? She didn't know what caused the accident, or if he knew he was going to be killed. Did he think of her and Leslie? Did he suffer? Crook had no answers.

Crook decided to carry on with her and her husband's dream to go to Ole Miss. In an unusual move for the time, this thirty-year-old single mother enrolled in college. Leslie was just five. Crook earned her degree and then she and Leslie moved to Waco, Texas, so Crook could take a job at the Veterans Administration Medical Center there. The patients were mentally ill, and Crook called upon her experiences at Marfa, where she had seen patients like this.

In 1958, Crook was remarried, to Henry Crook, a Chief Petty Officer who had a very successful career in the Navy, but she continued to work, which was unusual for married women in those days. Crook was devoted to her patients. She was heartbroken by those who were severely ill and had to be restrained. Some of these men, Crook thought, should never have gone to war.

Over the years, Crook always volunteered to work on Christmas and Thanksgiving, because she knew the patients needed her. Leslie understood that her mother needed to leave home for several hours on these days, realizing that these veterans, many of whom would never leave the hospital, needed her mother. Crook worked at the VA for twenty-five years, before retiring. "She lived what she believed, and she's a great example of what it means to be a member of a community. My mother taught me that freedom isn't free," Leslie says.

Leslie always felt different from the other kids, growing up with no father and a mom who worked a full-time job. For many years as a child, she believed that perhaps her father had survived the accident and would miraculously appear one day. Sometimes that happened in movies, she noticed. When she grew up, she learned about the nuclear experimentation that had been conducted on Eniwetok Atoll when her father was stationed there and about all the veterans who contracted cancer from the radiation poisoning. They are known as "Atomic Veterans," and the U.S. government has acknowledged their sacrifice and established a fund to help those who contracted cancer. Perhaps her father would have suffered from cancer if he had not died young, Leslie wonders.

Leslie and her mother finally felt a sense of closure about Leslie's father's death in December of 2007 when they went to Arlington National Cemetery and visited Jones' grave. An organization called Wreaths Across America, founded in 1992 by Morrill Worcester with the help of Maine Senator Olympia Snowe, raises funds to lay wreaths on the graves at Arlington. Leslie cannot express how deeply grateful she is to this organization. "They're honoring people like my daddy who have never been honored before. Now he won't be forgotten, which is the biggest fear," she explains. Leslie's children were able to honor their grandfather's grave, and the wreath laying ceremony that year was on December 15, coincidentally, the sixty-first anniversary of Jones' and Crook's romantic wedding in Biloxi. That trip inspired Leslie and her mother to contact the Air Force and request a copy of Jones' accident report.

In another coincidence, the accident report arrived in the mail at Crook's house on February 6, 2008, the anniversary of Jones' death. Mother and daughter read the report together, and Crook finally learned, after fifty-five years of worrying, that her husband had died immediately when his plane exploded. He had not suffered.

The report also revealed that the investigation into the accident had determined that the pilot's manual needed to be changed. The pilot who had hit Jones was practicing maneuvers, where pilots engage with each other, and didn't realize that Jones should not be engaged with as he was training for a mission and carrying explosives. The pilot's manual was changed to state that pilots must be thoroughly briefed before each training and practice mission as to what exactly they are permitted to do and exactly with whom they are to engage. Today, students say that the pilot's manual was written in blood.

Crook also was honored on a visit to Washington, D.C., in 2014 as a guest of Honor Flight Austin, which takes World War II veterans to visit the National World War II Memorial. Crook is deeply grateful for this honor and for how well she and the other veterans were treated on the trip. The people at Honor Flight Austin have announced that they are humbled by how much Crook and her family were asked to give to their country.

Crook's awards include the American Campaign Medal and the Good Conduct Award.

Sergeant Milton Krom

Krom fought on in Europe to Czechoslovakia, in Operation Neptune. He fought in the Battle of the Bulge. Krom fought from the early days of the war in Africa until the bitter end.

Krom went home "on points" in early May of 1945, just as Hitler was defeated and the war in Europe ended. Under the point system used for determining when servicemen and women could be discharged, points were earned for time served. Extra points were given for overseas and combat duty, for being injured and for having dependent children.

Krom remembers the men on the ship home cheering when the radio played a commercial in English, since that meant "we had gotten into waters near the U.S.," and later, more cheering as their ship steamed past the Statute of Liberty on May 5, his birthday. Krom was discharged about one month later, just before Japan surrendered in August and World War II came to an end.

Patriotic to the core, Krom continued to serve his country after his discharge, in the Army reserves. His wife Rose was terribly worried that he would have to go off to war again, in Korea, but he was not called up to deploy.

The summer he returned home, before the war ended, Krom took a job as an electrician at the Corbin Screw Division of the American Hardware Corporation and moved Rose and their two young sons to New Britain, Connecticut, where the company was located. He worked there until he retired.

Krom believes that if the U.S. had not prevailed on D-Day, it would have lost the war. The superb training the troops received, he believes, is what made D-Day a success. "It was our training that saved us. We did most of our maneuvers on the beach. Our training is what did it." Training had been intense – soldiers had practiced crawling on beaches under barbed wire with live fire overhead, for instance. Krom also gives credit to the men who, having lost their officers, were able to overcome the shock of the scene and rally the troops to move off the beach: "When we didn't have any officers, a sergeant would act as commanding officer. America does that. That doesn't happen with other countries."

Krom was one of more than 40,000 men who served in the 1st Infantry during World War II. Only half of them survived.

In the years since the war, he has struggled with awful memories of the terrible human suffering and death he saw in the war. He remembers the new, raw recruits late in the war being trucked out to the frontlines while trucks with American corpses "stacked like cordwood" drove past. "The new kids were so scared that they were crying, worried that they wouldn't make it," he recalls. Krom remembers one of his friends who was shot on four separate occasions. Each time, his gunshot wounds were treated, and he was sent back to the front lines to fight. One day, he stepped on a landmine and his leg was blown off. He was almost relieved, telling Krom, "Finally, they can't send me back anymore."

Seventy years later, Krom still dreams of seeing his buddies die awful deaths. He remembers watching his friends getting hit by explosives and burning to death. He empathizes with the servicemen and women of today. "People don't realize what it's like for them, seeing their friends getting blown up right before their eyes, by these roadside bombs," Krom says sadly. Krom can't get the pictures out of his mind, seventy years later. He is finally receiving treatment for Post Traumatic Stress Disorder. For years he was not treated because his caregivers believed that his nightmares and other emotional damage from the war were the result of the malaria he had contracted in Africa.

Like hundreds of thousands of wives during the war, Rose, who died in 1978, prayed for her husband constantly while he was overseas. She was very religious and went to church almost every day to light a candle for her husband. Krom feels that God was watching over him because of Rose's prayers, but he struggles with the question of why he survived when so many died. Krom has asked priests if they know why he lived when so many did not, and they tell him he may never know.

Krom has been strongly committed to community service since the war, in part to make his survival meaningful. He has remarried and currently lives in Florida with his wife Marie.

Krom's awards include the Bronze Star Medal; the World War II Victory Medal; the European, African and Middle Eastern Campaign Medal; and the Good Conduct Award.

Acknowledgements

Kristopher Perry, Lieutenant Colonel, Retired, U.S. Air Force, and Director, Office of Veterans Affairs and Military Programs at the University of Connecticut, was instrumental in getting this book started. Kris reviewed the first story, made the introductions to Mr. Boyer and Mr. Vendola, and provided tremendous encouragement over the course of this project. Kris, a graduate of the U.S. Naval Academy, retired after more than twenty years of active duty in the Navy and Air Force. He holds graduate degrees and is a veteran of multiple combat deployments, including Operation Enduring Freedom and Operation Iraqi Freedom. The Office of Veterans Affairs and Military Programs supports more than 1,200 veterans who are students at the University of Connecticut. Kris and his terrific staff are devoted to supporting the veterans enrolled at UConn.

For their help in finding veterans for this project and for their support and encouragement, many thanks to the following good people:

Bruce Allen, Sr., Commander of VFW Post 594 in Norwich, Connecticut and the Saturday breakfast group at the post; Todd Fairchild, of shutterbugct. com, a photographer whose father-in-law is Bill Cooke; Norma Carey, who enjoys learning about the war from her friend Ed Holopainen; Matt and Sarah Fitzsimons, devoted educators and son-in-law and daughter of Paul Lahr; Paul and Joan Frank, who stop by to see pals Bob and Shirley Poole when driving through Georgia; Frank and Mary ("Kathie") Bernard, who count Rudy and Doris Rolenz among their friends; Leslie Jones, proud daughter of Lois Crook and the late Clyde Ray Jones, Jr.; Deborah Geigis Berry, a gifted and compassionate editor and the great-niece of Sal Santoro; Brian Smith, Director, The Tuskegee Airmen National Historical Museum in Detroit, Michigan; Brad and Rhonda Astor, native Iowans and the nephew and niece-in-law of Jim Astor; Stacey Murphy, a Texas native whose uncle is Buck Lord; Bob and Linda Bertolette, devoted nephew and niece-in-law of the late Reed Bertolette; Larry Dunn, a much-loved son of the late Bud Dunn; Bob Barefield, who served as a Colonel in the U.S. Army in the Vietnam

War and is devoted to veterans' causes, including the Support Committee for the Alabama National Cemetery (scalnc.org), which serves military families; Pam Nichols of Honor Flight Birmingham; Dave Gemmel, who spends much of his free time honoring veterans; Mike Kadis, a Seabee who recently served in the Navy; Juanita Darling who worked hard to find veterans for this project and who is a big fan of the Navajo Code Talkers; Lisa Porter an educator who helped find an amazing war story; and Dr. Richard Colletti, proud father of a Marine.

Thanks to Dr. Ifeyinwa Onyiuke for her grace and inspiration; Amanda Sirica of Sirica Marketing & Public Relations for her generous mentoring, and Jim Tully, Publisher of Seasons Magazines, for affording me the privilege of writing for his smart, beautiful magazines over the past several years.

About the Title and Cover

Eleni Bouzakis, a friend and entrepreneur, suggested that a good title for this book might be a saying that was popular among the servicemen and women. On many occasions when I indicated to the veterans how impressive their feats and hardships throughout the war were, the veterans simply said, "We had a job to do."

Many veterans described their return from the War in Europe aboard troopships. When the Statue of Liberty came into sight, the troops would cheer and cry – they were home and safe. Sometimes the ship would tilt as everyone ran over to see the statue. Artist Kristin Bryant's cover for this book beautifully conveys the symbolism of the Statue of Liberty, the spirit of the times and the dedication of those who served.

On the back cover is a WAC recruiting poster, courtesy of the U.S. National Archives, and a photo of American infantrymen as they line up for chow in the snow on their way to LaRoche, Belgium, on January 13, 1945. Photographer Newhouse. Photo courtesy of the National Archives, number 111-SC-198849.

For more information and to see photos from the veterans, please visit theresaanzaldua.com.